PRAISE FOR

ABUNDANT
*soul*UTIONS

"Chris has helped me manifest all my dreams personally and professionally through the concepts she teaches in this book. As a couple who are both entrepreneurs, Chris has given us incredible guidance that has helped both of our different businesses. She has helped me reach clients I never thought would be possible!"
CASSIE AND FORD BLAKELY, founders of Warrior Parent Consulting and Zingle

"Chris's soul-centered approach to business has been such a huge help to me over the years. In her book, she shares how we can apply the 'real' law of attraction by actually loving and putting ourselves first. Chris's positivity and authentic straight talk is exactly what the world needs right now!"
SHARI OWEN BROWN, bestselling author and top network marketing leader

"I grew up in a culture where the people who work the most hours are the worthiest of success. When I met Chris, I was working like crazy and not getting results. It wasn't until I started working with her that I learned the help I needed most was with my self-love. My business quadrupled as a result, and the people around me also started to flourish. Her book will help you uncover what's holding you back and utilize the power of the universe that's already inside you, too!"

NAJLA WEHBE DIPP, global real estate agent and success coach

"Chris's empowering concepts and transformational process are truly a game changer in the world of fulfilling entrepreneurship. I've lived and breathed these concepts with the support and coaching from Chris. I've gone from spinning and spiraling to thriving and succeeding in ways that I could only have imagined. Chris reminds us that we already have the answers within, and that self-love is the key to unlocking the success that we're all searching and striving for."

NATALIE SCOTT, inspirational and business coach

ABUNDANT
*soul*UTIONS

www.amplifypublishinggroup.com

Abundant Soul-utions: A Mompreneur's Guide to Manifesting Success through Self-Care

For more information, please contact:
Amplify Publishing, an imprint of Amplify Publishing Group
620 Herndon Parkway, Suite 320
Herndon, VA 20170
info@amplifypublishing.com

Library of Congress Control Number: 2022919928

CPSIA Code: PRV0123A

ISBN-13: 978-1-63755-555-2

Printed in the United States

To all my friends, family, and mentors who stood by me while I was searching for the answers, your love and support was and is everything.

To my kids, Jude and Ella, I hope to always inspire you to take a stand for your dreams, and that you know you can have love and abundance in your life because of who you are on the inside.

To my husband, thank you for entertaining endless conversations with me on these topics!

———————

To you, amazing reader, may you know that you can be, do, and have anything in your life. You are limitless, and this book is for you!

ABUNDANT *soul*UTIONS

A MOMPRENEUR'S GUIDE TO MANIFESTING SUCCESS THROUGH SELF-CARE

CHRIS ATLEY

an imprint of Amplify Publishing Group

CONTENTS

INTRODUCTION

An Invitation from One Recovering Overachiever to Another

YOU'RE RUNNING A BUSINESS. You're a mother, a partner, a friend, *and* an active member in your community. You're doing *all* the things. Your mom has given you a gold star. People are thinking, "Wow, how can she do it all?" as you unconsciously sign up to make the Thanksgiving turkey for your kid's class.

Ugh.

What they're not seeing behind the scenes is that you are *hustling*—hustling to try to make your business work while making time for your family, friends, community, and not to mention *sexy time* with your spouse!

You've had success in your business and your career in your past life, but where your clients are coming from next is *unknown*. It's always been a grind to attract them and a constant source of *stress*. And you're tired, so very, very tired of hustling, trying to keep your home life thriving while keeping up with the latest trends on healthy eating and how to effectively potty train your kids.

Ugh.

Not to mention taking time for yourself and being *present!* Ugh again.

I hear you, and I *feel* you. This was me—yep, even the turkey part—and every now and then it still creeps in. *I come from a long line of hustlers*, like you probably do too. Not the illegal kind, but the women in my family are driven. We know how to hustle. We have a strong work ethic, and persistence runs in our genes. It was slightly embarrassing at my wedding when the minister mentioned not once but thrice how my husband loved my *drive*. I was like, "Isn't there anything else?" The poor guy didn't know what was coming as result of all this ambition.

My early days of *hustling* resulted in graduating high school a year early so that I could get on with university, to later defying the entrepreneurial odds and running multiple successful businesses while up and moving my family from Canada to the United States along the way. I had a drive and persistence like no other, and I was going to figure out the law of attraction and how to grow my business no matter what. But I was tired, overwhelmed, and burned out. I had learned a lot about self-care but wasn't quite *getting* it yet.

While I was growing up, my mom was anything but a stay-at-home mom (not that there's anything wrong with that!), determined to prove she could succeed in a male-oriented industry. After being the first in the family to get a university degree and later becoming a teacher, she also defied the odds by going on to become one of the best *salesmen* in the computer industry. She did the unthinkable and got divorced when I was four, despite all the societal *shoulds* and *should-nots* centred on marriage at the time. She was a force.

Even though all this was pretty much unheard of at the time, even more so was what her mom, my grandmother Dorothy, whom we lovingly called Gramma Dodie, did. She was a businesswoman who eventually worked her way up to running her own clothing store. She would go on buying trips to Toronto, where she stayed at the famous Royal York Hotel, which always seemed so glamorous. And it might sound like an upper-class situation, but it was modest at best. She struggled to succeed, like all of us. The common thread though? Three generations of defying odds and breaking through societal and gender stigmas.

That's what we're here to do in the pages to come: break through the stigmas.

Even though we've come a *long* way, with it being more acceptable for women to work outside the home, we're still off-kilter. We now have two jobs: running a household *and* navigating our careers. On top of us having careers, we chose entrepreneurship, which is not for the faint of heart. Owning and running a business takes determination, grit, and grace. Fortunately, the women who came before me had all three of these, and they imparted them upon me too. Entrepreneurship is no easy task. I always say it's the best personal development course one could ever take because we're forced to get out of our own way if we truly want to create the success we're seeking. It's 100 percent uncomfortable—insert added stress—and 200 percent worth it.

And underneath the entrepreneurial highs and lows also lie the potential mental and physical health concerns. Not only can these issues be very limiting and even debilitating for us as business owners but also just think about how far-reaching these issues can go, extending out to our families, clients, communities, and countries.

All because entrepreneurship promised us we could *have it all*: be home with the kids *and* run a business—translation: be a good mom *and* still contribute to your household.

But sadly, it has been reported by multiple sources that one in five female entrepreneurs have contemplated suicide, a quarter have reported mental health issues, and 50 percent of small businesses do not survive beyond five years.

This has to change.

And not only change but we also need to know *how to flourish*.

What if it actually *is possible* to not only survive but also thrive, where results flow, where we have compassionate relationships, and where life is lived to the fullest? What kind of world would that be?

As we will learn in the pages of this book, all this *is* possible . . . through the counterintuitive pathway of self-care.

Where we are finally taught to give ourselves permission to take care of ourselves first and how this has a profound and enduring ripple effect for our families, friends, and finances.

Abundant Soul-utions shows female entrepreneurs that they actually can have it *all*; it just involves redefining what all looks like and reevaluating the *how* of getting there.

And don't worry, we're not getting rid of *hustling* entirely, because it's served us well; we're just going to transform it into *inspired action*, drop the deep-rooted fear driving it, and replace it with manifesting from a place of happiness instead.

After spending thousands of hours coaching female entrepreneurs and sorting through my own *stuff* for the last sixteen-plus years, I unintentionally became an expert in the entrepreneurial mind, specifically for women—where it gets tripped up, where it gets stuck, and unfortunately (or fortunately, depending on how you look at it), where it goes down a deep, dark spiral. Thankfully, I've also learned how we can learn to pull ourselves out of those spirals, make empowered decisions, and manifest our biggest, boldest dreams instead.

When I first learned the concept that we can be, do, and have anything in life, I took the bull by the horns to figure this stuff out because I knew, in the depths of my core, it was the *truth*. I up and moved my family to the United States, where I fulfilled a lifelong dream of living by the beach. Thank goodness my husband was on board, but honestly, that, too, was part of the visualization process.

Even though I learned about self-care early on in my coaching career, with it actually helping me *create* my coaching business, I still didn't fully grasp it. Self-care helped me become *nicer* because I became a happier person, but I was still missing the mark. Self-care, although helpful, had become just another *to-do* on the never-ending to-do list. I found I was rushing all day and moving through the motions, especially with my kids, to get to the place of finally being able to relax at the end of the day. And, ladies, this was with a supportive husband. (More on that later.) But I found myself either falling asleep in my kids' bed while trying to get them to go to sleep or almost instantaneously falling asleep when my head hit the pillow in my own bed. Forget that personal development time I told my coach I would take.

And I was hustling. Man, did I know how to hustle. I would not stop until I was successful. I would not stop no matter what self-imposed goal I put on myself. This looked like hiring endless coaches and belonging to mastermind groups, both mindset and marketing related (I was doing online marketing before

Facebook was even a thing. Remember teleclasses?), along with reading everything I could get my hands on about the law of attraction, because I *knew* deep down that this was the truth, that we can use our minds to create our reality. Rest assured, there is more on that to come.

It was this tight grip I had around my goals and lifetime dreams that was actually pushing them away. Success still came in, but it always came with struggle and stress. Not quite what I had imagined when I started my business. It did not flow with ease, the way I knew, intuitively, that it could.

What changed? I finally got the true *secret*. What we put out always comes back, including stress and anxiety. I realized I was operating from a place of fear deep down—fear of where the next clients would come from, fear of not doing enough, fear of not being smart enough, and fear of running out of time. I was coming from a place of *lack*, essentially, where there was never *enough* of something. And what I didn't realize until later was that I was always searching for the answers outside myself. My *good enough* sparkled from afar, always teasing me with one more course or one more program, with the promise of success. But my deep-seated belief of *not enoughness* actually kept the success I was wanting at arm's length. Until it didn't. And don't get me wrong, all the training and courses I took served a very useful purpose and taught me valuable information that I needed to know. But the ultimate lesson was learning to trust myself and tune in to my own intuition.

When we tackle the deep-seated (and often misguided) beliefs we accepted to be true in our past, we will learn what is driving our decisions currently, in both our businesses and personal lives. This is where the phrase "get comfortable being uncomfortable" comes into play because it's uncomfortable to acknowledge and change the way we've been operating for an entire lifetime. Letting go of thought systems that have seemed safe can be scary at first. It's this discomfort that a lot of people aren't willing (or able) to move through. But you are here, you are holding this book in your hands, and you are ready. And I can promise you, if you stick with it, the freedom and liberation that lie on the other side is 1,000 percent worth it. Living an abundant life, a life that we love.

Does it mean tough stuff doesn't happen and we just *love and light* everything?

No.

But it does mean you will have the tools and awareness to handle things when they do come up with much more ease. Permission to feel is half the battle. Permission to tune in to your own needs is the other half. With permission in and of itself generating a powerful ripple effect of grace and compassion out to the universe.

It's as simple, and as hard, as operating from an empowered place. It's where *enoughness* lies. Where we are operating at such a high vibrational energy that we literally see all the solutions there for us. Where we are our most resourceful and where we can become a limitless version of ourselves. Where we allow ourselves to receive all the goodness that the universe has to offer. Where we truly can do what we love in *all* areas of life. Where there aren't any trade-offs, because we're doing what we love *across the board*. And this *flow* I'm referring to starts and finishes with self-care and not about sacrificing anything in between.

It's my intention that by the end of this book you will not

only have practical tools for putting the *you* back into your business and creating happiness and peace but that you also truly understand, and are seeing evidence of, how self-care will take you to your highest heights, to your most limitless you, and to your ultimate success. Whatever success looks like for you and only you.

Because I can tell you without a doubt, with running multiple businesses, speaking around the world, living in my dream spot, all the while attending my kids' activities and being present for them when they need me, that we can truly be, do, and have anything in life. This is much easier and simpler than we think. The universe doesn't say, "I get to follow my dreams, and you don't." But it absolutely does ask you to step up and ask for what you want. It absolutely does ask you to tune in to what you love and connect with what makes you happy. It absolutely does ask you to let go of limiting beliefs and align yourself with self-love and worthiness.

In this book, I will do a deep dive into all these areas. As a result of this personal work, I've been honoured to coach amazing humans, to be featured in the media, to write for publications, to give a TEDx talk in India, to create lucrative coaching and real estate investing companies, and to even host a podcast with my best friend on one of my favourite topics—A Course in Miracles. All because I figured this stuff out with relentless perseverance. While it is not about accomplishments, it *is* about creating our heart's desires. We are meant to cocreate a life we love with whom we love. May my lessons be your springboard.

The concepts I share in my TEDx talk (chrisatley.com/tedx) will be the cornerstone of what we do together here in the pages to come. How the best version of ourselves is what will actually help us manifest the empowered results and the lifestyle we're looking for. It all starts within, and when this is extended out to the world, we create a far-reaching, world-changing ripple effect. I will also take you through the exact processes that I've taken thousands of people through, which will help you completely transform your life and business. We deserve to move from stress, fear, doubt, and worry to a place of confidence, peace, love, and abundance.

As we start our journey together, here is a quick description of some of the topics we'll be exploring:

* A shiny gem awaits you, but the water is too murky to see right now. We are going to give you an upgraded mask, snorkel, *and* flashlight so that you can shine a light on the beliefs keeping you in a disempowered way of *be*-ing. You cannot truly move forward until you've healed. Otherwise, those lessons will continue to pop up. It's what is steering the ship, and it's what is behind procrastination. Once we awaken our inner guidance system, we can consciously create the results we're wanting. Now *that* is true empowerment.

* Self-care is not self-*ish*; it's self-*less*. We are going far deeper than a mani-pedi (although those can be great too) to build a solid foundation of self-care as a way of *be*-ing that lends to deeper connections and being of service on a far more impactful level.

* Imagine being so clear that you actually create more time for yourself. Okay, time exists in equal increments for everyone, but when we examine our choices around it and make conscious decisions instead, we actually free up more

of it. Evaluating your *inner junk drawer* will allow you to clear out the clutter in your relationships, environments, finances, and health and emotional well-being. It's what will enable you to take back your power and do more of what you love.

* Why do you say yes when you want to say no? This is hands down the issue I see business owners struggling with the *most*, and it creeps in at *all* levels. When we address the history of people-pleasing and get clear on our own values, we set ourselves free while setting boundaries with love and respect, of course. For ourselves and others.

* When you become conscious of choosing your own thoughts, you will be amazed at how you let go of the expectations others have of you and the self-imposed limitations you're putting on yourself.

* Ever wonder why you're constantly comparing yourself with others and coming up short? Introducing the ego—the epidemy of never enoughness. We are going to take a deep dive into this beast and examine how it's formed and how to choose *differently*. It cannot survive in the light, even though it's there lurking around every corner, waiting to pounce.

* When you're trying to be perfect, whose approval is it you're so desperately looking for? So many of us are seeking love and approval outside ourselves, but when we take the time to consciously tune in, become confident in who we are, and really see ourselves truthfully, we see that we are *ah*-mazing, regardless of our achievements. Society has taught us to look outside ourselves for this validation, but we're going to flip the switch and go *within*. Freedom alert!

* You are not a victim to your circumstances. You get to design a life you love, on your terms. We are going to harness the most important universal laws and provide a road map that shows you the steps you need to follow to fully bring them to fruition. Get ready to learn the mind-blowing correlation to self-care.
* Still holding on to a grudge? No worries. I've got you. It's integral to your success that we explore forgiveness. What it actually is and how to practice it. Clients have been known to skyrocket their businesses after practicing forgiveness. Who would have thought?
* You deserve to be a lighter, more resourceful, loving, calm version of yourself. Where anything and everything is possible. Where you are tuned in, confident, and clear in your decision-making. A place where you and your intuition are a force to be reckoned with. This is where true *limitless* lies, and you will come to see that abundance already lies inside you.

I have been studying self-care for the last seventeen years—before it was even a *thing*—and I am convinced it's my life lesson. I learned the intricate details on what it really means to practice self-care and create a life and business that puts it at the forefront. It's counterintuitive to what we've been taught, and we're going to change that. When we step into this place of putting our own needs and emotional well-being at the forefront, the universe not only sees us but also raises us.

We're going to flip these social norms on their head, challenge ourselves, and come out freer than we've ever felt before. Where opportunities and *soul*-utions are plentiful. Where you have an empowered thought, and the inspired next step simultaneously shows up, all as a result of practicing self-care on this deeper, multifaceted level. And what's interesting is that out of the thousands of business owners I have taken through the empowered lifestyle exercise, when they map out their big lifestyle dreams, it always comes back to self-care being the way to get them there. It's like we all intuitively know this is the way. Love attracts love, and the magic of the universe never ceases to amaze me. I am going to take you through this exercise, too, in the second chapter.

Let's make the commitment to pull back the curtain, clear out the cobwebs, and start living full out. No one is going to take a stand for you except you. I will be with you every step of the way and cannot wait for you to see what you are capable of creating.

So take my hand and join me on this journey.

We'll start at the beginning, by examining the power of belief.

Love,
Chris xox

1

HAM IN THE PAN

The Power of Beliefs

YOU'RE NOT ALONE IN FEELING the enormous pressure that comes with running a business and juggling a family, trying to keep up with the PTA, providing an abundant life for your kids, while trying to prove you have a legitimate, thriving business! Switching hats from mom to wife to boss babe (what even *is* that?) is exhausting, to say the least. We have somehow taken on the role of master manager of the universe, and we believe this is *normal*, just the way it is. We convince ourselves into thinking, "If I don't do it, no one will," and "If I want anything done right, I have to do it myself."

This mentality is based on years of untruths we have been sold, passed down from society, our cultures, and the influential people in our lives. We've been taught that we *have* to do it all, and we have to do it with a smile on our faces. We believe that running a household and a business is the ultimate freedom and that when we accomplish both, we *should* be happy. We've earned the right to be here after all, and these are *champagne* problems compared with other things going on in the world. And so we stay quiet, we keep the peace, while silently suffering underneath (and in the midst of) it all.

It's time to change our thinking. We need to realize we've been sold a big fat lie. A long line of women's rights is getting us to the place of equality, but is it actually even equal? To me, it sounds like two jobs resting on *our* shoulders. And honestly, it's not anyone's fault, because it came with good intentions; we wanted and do want to be treated equally. But we haven't levelled the playing field just yet. We now feel the heaviness of two *jobs* on our shoulders, where we think it's normal and just the way it is. But what if this is just a long line of beliefs, stemming from women being taught way back in the day that they are responsible for maintaining the *home*? Where they are shamed and shunned if they're not doing this. What if we are unconsciously making decisions from this place? Or worse, what if we *want* to make decisions deep down from this place? What if it's a way for us to feel safe and in control? To feel loved and valued? Either way, there is an underlying belief system simmering just beneath the surface that dictates how we should show up in *all* areas of life.

The "ham in the pan" story is always a crowd-pleaser with my audiences, whether I'm coaching large groups, working one-on-one with people, or delivering a keynote speech, because it drives home the power of beliefs. A husband and wife are preparing a ham, and the wife cuts off the ends of the ham. The husband asks her why she does it this way, and she replies that she isn't sure, she's just *always* done it this way, and that's how her mom prepares it. When they take this same question to her mom and ask why she prepares the ham this way, her response is virtually the same. She also says she isn't sure, that she's just *always* done it this way. So the curious couple takes things one step further and asks the wife's grandma why she cuts the ends off a ham when preparing it. The grandma laughs and says, "Oh, that's easy . . . because the pan was too small!"

And therein lies the truth. We do not question why we believe what we do. We just do it.

Until now.

Beliefs are ideas we have accepted to be true that have been passed down from generation to generation through societies, religions, and cultures. We generally don't question them; we just assume they're rooted in the truth. With even the belief of not questioning our elders and *doing as we're told* coming from a set of beliefs in and of itself. A belief is formed when we accept the information we're receiving, whether it's true or not. In turn, our beliefs guide how we perceive others, how we behave (or don't behave) in specific situations, and how we interact with the world around us. Beliefs are the lens through which we see the world; they determine every single decision we make. The way we see the world is the cornerstone of our decision-making and in turn dictates the actions we take or don't take. In a very real way then, our belief system holds great power in the life we create for ourselves.

The issue is that most of these beliefs stem from our subconscious mind, meaning we are often not aware of them. Many in the scientific community estimate that 95 percent of our brain activity happens in our subconscious mind, meaning the majority of the decisions we make and the actions we take lie beyond our conscious awareness. We just do what we do without much question or reflection because we've already accepted our behaviour as right and therefore true. We run on autopilot.

Let's explore our subconscious mind a little further. This is the part of our brain that does not have the ability to reject or accept information. Beliefs are accepted to be true in the subconscious mind through consistent repetition, such as seeing how a ham is prepared over and over, and also through any emotional reactions we have to the world and the people in it. Think about all the beliefs we have around money, success, and our roles (and perceived roles) within the world. For most, these beliefs are very limited at best, all stemming from ideas we accepted to be true during our youth without even realizing it.

Our conscious mind, on the flip side, has the ability to reason and can therefore accept or reject information. It's the part of us that has free will, where we can think, "No, that doesn't sound right" or "Yes, that sounds accurate." Then we can decide to reject or accept the information accordingly. Research shows that the conscious mind is not formed until around the age of seven years old, meaning we don't have the ability to accept or reject information *at all* until the conscious mind is formed. We are pretty much just accepting everything to be true. And hold on, moms, I know what you're thinking: "Shoot, I have royally screwed up my kids!" I felt the same, but my thinking has since evolved. Now I appreciate the fact that our kids have their own lessons to learn and overcome, and it's just not up to us to determine what exactly those are. Whenever we learn this information is the exact right time, and *how* we use it moving forward is what counts. We want to get to the place of *consciously* choosing what information we accept or reject and decide for *ourselves* what we believe—and therefore allow into our subconscious mind as a result. Most people do not know they can do this. But I am here to tell you that you *can*!

It's important to note that it's not so much that the subconscious mind is bad; it's simply doing its job, protecting us and keeping us *safe*. We all innately know to run away from a tiger, and that's because we've accepted this truth subconsciously through the information presented to us growing up. The issue is that when we put ourselves out there in the world of business, we do not feel safe deep down. Putting ourselves out in front of others and, dare I say, *asking for the sale* just doesn't feel safe; if anything, there are feelings of vulnerability and doubt that come along with asking for that sale and closing that deal. Agreed?

When we are in vulnerable situations, warning bells go off in our subconscious mind, and it will do anything and everything to keep us safe. It makes sense that this is also behind much of our procrastination. Our subconscious mind keeps us from tasks that make us feel uncomfortable, which is most business growth activities, and this part of our mind will literally create thought patterns that get us to stop. To pull back. To hesitate. To make a different decision, such as doing busy work instead. But staying small and stunted does not contribute to our growth and development, either financially or emotionally. If we listen to our subconscious mind that so often tells us, "Wait until you have more energy," or "You don't need to do that now," we will end up closing down our businesses or, worse, allowing the stress of not reaching our financial goals to compromise our mental or physical health. To be sure, our subconscious knows *exactly* how to pull us back, slow us down, and redirect our path, even if that new path is exciting, adventurous, and potentially profitable.

I'll use myself as an example. Earlier in my career, when I was trying to get ahead in the business world, my own subconscious mind loved to tell me that I was too tired to go to an important networking event, for instance, even though I knew deep down that attending that event would help me, or that I wasn't in the *perfect* energy to make sales calls, which often led me to stop trying. (Remember: thoughts dictate behaviour.)

This is where we need to push through. We need to understand our subconscious mind, to be vitally aware of what it's trying to do and realize the moments when it might be leading us down the wrong path (or even down a circuitous path that will not contribute to our growth). Stop. You are capable of retraining your brain and heightening your own awareness. Once I learned to do this, I actually started to *enjoy* sales calls and truly saw them as a way of helping people.

This simple exercise might help: Take a pause. Reflect upon, evaluate, and then write down every area you're currently struggling with and avoiding in your business. Create a list. Take a careful look at your *stuck points*, at those points where you *know* that taking a certain action will lead to your success, but you somehow stop yourself from taking that step. Good job. Congratulate yourself here because this first, all-important step of heightening your awareness is crucial.

Unfortunately, becoming aware of how the subconscious mind operates is not enough though. It's important, certainly, but it is not enough by itself. We also need to look at the beliefs we have formed that the subconscious mind is operating from. If we can up-level and perhaps even reimagine our definition of what *safe* is, we will have taken the first important step towards reprogramming our subconscious mind. We will have taken ourselves a step closer to becoming comfortable with discomfort.

It's where the phrase "Get comfortable being uncomfortable"

comes into play. It's uncomfortable to pull back the curtain and look at what is making us feel the way we do. Whether it's an old childhood memory causing these feelings or a long-standing family pattern we've just accepted to be true. Either way, there is an unease that occurs when we start disrupting patterns we have been accepting to be true for such a long time.

Once we are aware of the origin of these feelings and how they are impacting our lives, we can't *not* address them. If we want to create a new, empowered result, we have to make new and empowered choices, which is very uncomfortable, especially if they impact important people in our lives. Disrupting these dynamics creates a real threat inside us. Most people stop here. If we keep going, though, and learn how to make these choices with as much grace as possible, we not only become liberated but we also give others permission to do the same. When we keep raising the bar on our discomfort level, it's no longer uncomfortable. It's just a way of *be*-ing.

This story from my high school days will illustrate both what an emotional reaction is and how the subconscious mind uses it to keep us safe. When I was growing up in Canada, we were all required to take advanced classes in high school if we wanted to continue on with a postsecondary degree versus going to a community college. And even though there is nothing wrong with community college, in my family, it wasn't a question of *if* I would go to university; it was *when* I was going. Not going was not an option.

One memory stands out especially. I was in a science class in grade nine and wasn't doing especially well. My teacher called my mom and me in for a meeting, and basically, what I heard was that I *wasn't smart enough* to continue on in advanced science and needed to drop down a level. Thank goodness my mom believed I could pass that class, and thank goodness I also had a strong will to succeed.

My teacher's attempts to get me to drop down a level were just what I needed to get motivated. I remember thinking, *Your class is boring, but I will just start paying attention.* I was a big daydreamer, with school never quite captivating my interest. I stayed in the advanced science class, and not only did I pass but I also continued on with advanced-level classes in both science and my other subjects and did just fine. More than fine, actually, graduating with an A average and getting into a top university in Canada, going on to obtaining a bachelor's degree in psychology.

Still, though, a part of me accepted what my teacher said to be true. It was hurtful to think I wasn't smart enough to stay in the class, and that left a mark. An imprint, if you will. Even though logically (and academically) speaking it wasn't true, her comments and observations still stung, and I carried that pain inside me for quite some time. What hurts, hurts. Emotions are real, and they have a way of sinking into one's psyche and becoming beliefs (or semibeliefs) without our even recognizing it.

Let me explain. A part of me reacted to my teacher's words, and a belief around *not enough* was formed. I would learn later on in my entrepreneurial days just how much this belief would hinder my success. This mistaken belief that I had allowed to become imprinted in my mind actually went on to dictate a whole bunch of decisions as I moved forward in life, such as what I studied in university. I decided to take a minor in business but never quite felt as smart as the *honour* business students. Wilfrid Laurier University was known for its business school, and I was surrounded by these superbright humans. As soon as the going got tough—insert an economics class I could not for the life of me understand—I gave up on that path, always feeling *less than*.

How ironic that I would one day run my own successful business rooted in studying human behaviour! So even though my subconscious kept me stuck in a place of self-doubt and maybe even fear, I made the conscious decision to take control of my subconscious thinking, employing my strong will to succeed as the mechanism that would move me forward. So yes, subconscious thinking is strong, but our ability to turn that thinking around can be even stronger. I am living proof.

Here's another example of that same belief that was hindering me: I began my first job (career) four days after getting my degree. And even though I excelled at moving up quickly with getting the certifications I needed—and promotions—I was still plagued by this nasty, nattering voice telling me that I wasn't smart enough.

I'll never forget being at a meeting once with my female boss. We were the only two women in the room, not all that uncommon in this primarily male-dominated industry. When it was my turn to weigh in on an issue, she stared at me, and I could feel her telepathically *willing* me to speak up. I sat there silently, too uncomfortable to speak up and deathly afraid of being judged by the important executives in the room. This was inert decision-making and failure to act, both coming from a subconscious mind that was trying to keep me safe.

My boss was so mad she barely spoke to me after that. I'm not sure if she ever fully forgave me, and who knows how that impacted her decisions towards me. She did pull me into her office a few months later, telling me not to be afraid of being a b-i-t-c-h when needed. That's sad, right? That was the only way women felt they could get ahead with men. Talk about limiting belief systems.

Fast-forward to my early entrepreneurial days, when I had been running a coaching business for a few years already. I started looking at why I wasn't at the level I knew I could be, why I wasn't growing and advancing at a more rapid rate. My business had plateaued, and it didn't matter how many courses I took or mastermind groups I belonged to; the fact of the matter was that I was not getting the results I knew I was capable of.

I had watched the movie *The Secret* and agreed, deep down, with its premise that we can all be, do, and have anything in life. I finally tuned in that I was the *common denominator* in all the trainings I took and that something was off with *me*! This was when I really started studying belief systems, and it was then and only then that I realized I did not feel smart enough. Translation: not good enough. Translation: lacking in some way.

I was *seeing* through this lens and subconsciously making decisions from this weakened, compromised place, which cor-related directly with my lagging results. This belief was safe and comfortable and my subconscious mode of apparatus. It didn't know anything was wrong. It wasn't out to get me. It was just operating the way it was programmed to. It wasn't until I started examining my belief systems—really, truly, deeply examining my belief systems—that everything started to flow. And quickly! With tripling my income in the first few months and growing it ten times in just ten months! It was like I was finally seeing the missing piece. And it had nothing—I repeat, *nothing*—to do with the strategy. I knew that inside and out.

We have to start using our conscious mind to shine a light on the beliefs that we've accepted to be true (either through consistent repetition or emotional reactions), that live in our subconscious mind.

Our conscious mind can therefore be used to pull back the veil and shine a light on what is hiding out in our subconscious mind. Which beliefs are running the show? Which are responsible for how we run households to how we run businesses? How did they seep into our subconscious minds, and what do we want to believe moving forward? Answer these questions, and you will start to write a new story, a new narrative that belongs to you and you alone! One where we become aware of those disempowered beliefs that are limiting our true happiness. Where we can flip the script and write a new *empowered* story moving forward. Where we truly are inspired cocreators. To create an empowered life we love, we need an empowered operating system to support it.

I was working with a client once who had plateaued in her marketing business. She was feeling very uncomfortable having sales conversations, as most of us do when running a business. She was having a lot of anxiety whenever it came to approaching a sale, which was, of course, blocking the growth of her business.

When we are in business for ourselves, we are also, by definition, in sales. Nobody wants to feel like they're being *sold to*, and deep down, most of us don't want to be that type of person. But she and I did the exercise I will take you through soon, and what we discovered was astonishing.

Her memory took her back to a time when she was a little girl. Her mom was a prominent member of society and held a leadership position in their town. They were at an event when she was about three or four years old, and she remembered, during the exercise, that doughnuts were served. She was eating a doughnut but didn't want the rest of it. There was a plant nearby, and she thought she would hide the remainder of the doughnut in the planter because she didn't want it anymore.

Without realizing her mom was watching, she reached over to drop it in the planter, and all of a sudden, her hand was slapped. Her mom reprimanded her for discarding the doughnut. In that moment, she made the very important decision that to get her mother's love and approval, she needed to stay quiet. She needed to do as she was told and be a good girl.

Years and years later, as we were to discover, this subtle but powerful decision to stay quiet and to be obedient was hindering her ability to reach out to others in order to grow her business. It made sense that she therefore would have extreme anxiety anytime she went to do this. Why? Because it was disrupting this deep-down need and deeply ingrained pattern to gain love and approval, so any action that she took that would interrupt this pattern was *threatening*. Through deeper work, we were able to help her redefine what having love and approval for herself actually meant, and by strengthening this new belief, she was able to grow her business quickly and actually started *enjoying* sales calls. They are about helping people after all.

With our beliefs being at the core of every decision we make, it is imperative that we do the *deeper dive* that is required to address which beliefs are actually steering our ship. Remember that we are the captain of our ship. We have the capacity to shine a light on the beliefs that are anchoring us down and causing us to sink, whether in our business lives or in our personal lives.

Understand that there is not a neat, clearly marked line of separation between our personal lives and our business lives either. No. *All* areas of our lives are interconnected. And it's not until we become aware of the limiting beliefs running the show that we can shift them to empowered beliefs. It's all about the state of mind (feeling) we are operating from. We have now pulled back the curtain, and we want to keep doing so. Start questioning why you believe what you believe in *all* areas of your life.

Let's dive in! What is behind the grind and the constant anxiety? What is driving that relentless pace of life where we hustle, grind, and *do*? Where, when we do achieve a goal, we add in *more* because it's *never* quite enough? We trick ourselves into believing that someday we will relax once we've reached a certain level. But sadly, that *someday* never comes. We just keep piling on more to that never-ending to-do list and adding new items to our goal-achieving extravaganza. It's kind of become an addiction and as far away as possible from the true freedom we're really craving. All because we are trying to keep up with those old belief systems that are swirling like a dark current deep down in our subconscious minds.

I'm going to take you through an exercise in which we will discover the limiting belief that is likely keeping you in this overwhelmed, less-than-stellar place. It's not necessarily a *bad* place, but it *is* preventing you from living a fully empowered life. This might sound familiar: you know more is possible for you, more growth is waiting for you, but you are feeling stuck. Well, this exercise will help you get unstuck. It's the one exercise I truly wish everyone in the world could do—business owner, parent, student, whatever your role in life. This exercise helps us see (and understand) the beliefs behind why we do what we do, and if nothing else, it will hopefully give you the awareness to change.

I do want to mention, at the outset, that what comes up will likely be uncomfortable. But just remember this: your dreams lie on the other side of this discomfort. We are going to identify what is going on beneath the surface. It's important to discover where the belief came from and how it was formed to use this awareness to let go of the power it has over us, but we don't want to dwell on the why of beliefs, because that in itself can keep us stuck. Let's set the intention that we are going to use this work as an awareness tool and that it's about moving forward and not dwelling on the past. We just want to become aware of it so that we can then *shift* it.

COACH APPROACH

I am going to take you through an exercise. If you would like to be led via audio, please visit my resources page at chrisatley. com/bookresources.

First, choose a comfortable, private area where you have the freedom to move around.

Next, go ahead and create three spots on the ground. This first one represents your empowered lifestyle, where everything you want to create is already there for you. Where you can dream big and have it all. People tend to choose an area in the room that feels good for them, like a lighter spot by the window. Choose a spot in the room that you are drawn to. Good job!

Now decide on the second spot in the room, one that represents a disempowered future. It's not necessarily *bad* but a future where you continue as is, where it's more of the same, and where you're not quite doing what you want to be doing or living the way you want to be living. Choose a spot in the room that represents this future for you. Good. Let's also create a third neutral spot on the floor, where when you stand in it, you can observe both the empowered and disempowered spots in the room. Excellent job!

Next, grab a notebook and pen. Now move into the neutral spot on the floor, and actually physically move your body so that you are standing in that spot. From this neutral place, look at the empowered future first, where everything you want to create has already happened. Do not step into it yet, but just *look* at it and think about what that type of a future looks like for you; get a clear picture of it in your mind. Good. Now look at the disempowered future, and do the same thing. Don't step into it, but by just looking at it, get a clear picture of what that disempowered way of operating looks like for you. Good job.

Go ahead and physically step into this disempowered future on the floor with your pen and paper. It's probably pretty familiar here. I want you to ask yourself the following questions, and write them down in your notebook while you're standing in this spot:

1. What is it like here? How does it feel? Think about all the feelings coming up in this place. Has your heart rate increased? Have your breathing patterns changed? What physical manifestations are occurring? Where do you feel them in your body? Write them down. Take careful note.

2. What thoughts do you tell yourself in this place? What is the main belief you have that keeps you here? What is it you're believing to be true that keeps you operating in this place? Beliefs about yourself, the important people in your life, the world in general. Write it all down.

3. Step into the neutral spot on the floor for a few breaths. While looking at the disempowered space, check in and see if there is any more information to be had on what keeps you there. Summarize in one sentence the main belief that keeps you operating in the disempowered place. Write it down. Great job.

4. Step back into the disempowered spot on the ground. What is the main feeling you feel here? What is one word that describes this feeing? Make sure it is the predominant feeling, the root of all other feelings. Close your eyes, and allow this feeling to take you back in time to your earliest memory of feeling it. Go with whatever memory and age that pops up. Anything goes. What was going on at that time? Summarize it in your mind. What important decisions did you make about yourself as a result? About the people involved? About the world in general, if that is important? Then ask yourself what the positive intention was for forming those decisions. What were they designed to do? Write down all the decisions you made and the positive intentions.

5. Allow your adult self to go back in time and have a pep talk with this younger version of yourself. Go back in time to just before the incident in question occurred. Just envision the conversation happening. Have your older self share all the truth and wisdom they have to lend your younger self

about handling this incident. Also, have your older self share any knowledge, information, and tools that will help this younger version of yourself thrive throughout life in general. Good job. Write down the main things that your adult self shared with your younger self.

6. Be this younger version of yourself who was just given this pep talk, and fully embrace this knowledge as the truth with a few deep breaths. Now bring this knowledge with you as you travel through your life, and come back to the present day. Notice how your life has shifted as you come back to now. You are likely feeling lighter, as though a burden has been lifted. Tune in and notice how this shift will help you move forward in both your life and business.

7. Physically step back into the neutral spot on the floor. Which future would you rather have? If it's the empowered future, let's move forward. If not, ask yourself another question. What are you afraid to let go of? Write it down. When you have firmly chosen the empowered future, you are ready to continue. It is there waiting for you, and we are ready to start bringing it to fruition. Woo hoo!

Congratulations! You have now identified the limiting belief that keeps you operating in a disempowered way, like the client with the planter. You are also now aware of where this belief came from. Although there was a positive intention for these decisions at that time, these beliefs are no longer serving you and are keeping you confined to being a more limited version of yourself. Start to notice anytime you feel yourself being pulled over to the disempowered space. Stop. Acknowledge it.

Breathe into it. Remind yourself it is from an old story no longer serving you, and make a note of what is triggering you to go back there. It could be a thought, a person, or even something in your environment. Revisit the pep talk that your adult self gave you often. This is consistent repetition.

2

DON'T LET THE POOL GO GREEN

Self-Care Is Selfless

I ATTENDED A WOMEN'S ENTREPRENEURIAL event years ago, and I will never forget what one of the speakers said: "Don't let the pool go green," meaning don't get so far down the entrepreneurial rabbit hole that you lose sight (a.k.a. control) of everything around you. The message was that it's *okay* if some things are left undone, such as the laundry, but don't get so far off track that you spin out of control and miss the important things, such as feeding your child! I loved this at the time. Permission *granted* to let things slide, especially during an era in which *work-life balance* was gaining traction.

I used this phrase as a talk title for years and longed to be on an entrepreneurial panel sharing my thoughts about the concept itself. Well, fast-forward and here I am today, teaching, speaking, and writing on this topic, and I've also been on a few panels over the years too. Little did I know, when I first heard the phrase all those years ago, that it would open the door for a much bigger conversation around self-care.

I realized along the way that the phrase work-life balance is just another *perfection* trap. Have everything go seamlessly at work and home—a.k.a. going perfectly, neat and tidy. Translation: *impossible*! What does being perfect mean anyway? Having it all together? Never missing a school function for our kids or the opportunity to volunteer in their class? Being a badass boss babe at work getting it *all* done? Always being in a good mood? Never making a mistake? It's just not possible. We are human, and life is messy. I used to get so upset by what I perceived as the *imbalances* that would creep into my life; just when I would think everything was flowing, one of my kids would get sick and throw a *wrench* into my beautifully orchestrated plan. What I've come to learn, though, is that the more time we take for ourselves, the more we can handle life's curveballs. We are more patient, loving, and giving with others *and* ourselves.

On that note, how many of us would like to operate beyond *not letting the pool go green*? Where we can have any darn colour or shade we want? Preferably beautiful, sparkly blues for me, please!

But seriously, why not a world where *we* are in charge of creating the experiences we want? Whether it's snuggling with our kids when they don't feel well or (gasp) letting the housework slide? Better yet, how about allowing ourselves to do exactly what makes us happy? Where we grant ourselves permission to fill up our *own* cup first and *then* give to others from the overflow? A world where we are happy, relaxed, and having fun again *even* when life throws us a curveball? Where letting life's curveballs roll off our backs *is* true work-life balance.

What does *that* look like?

I've been studying self-care for a long time now, and it has been a crazy, unexpected evolution. The life lesson that I've learned is that the more I take care of myself, the more everything around me flows positively, from business to my relationships. And funny enough, my coaching career actually started with self-care and is actually what sold me on doing it professionally.

About halfway into my insurance career, I started feeling *stuck*. I was handling large property and liability claims for companies such as Pepsi, the Home Depot, and even the province of Ontario prison system. I loved it when I felt I was helping people, but it eventually became unnerving, seeing people at their worst in such an adversarial system. After a few years of soul-searching and almost going back to school for a master's degree either in psychology or business administration, with neither feeling quite right, I discovered coaching. As I mentioned earlier, I'd recently watched the movie *The Secret*, which is about realizing and attaining every good thing you want in your life through your thoughts, and the timing was not a coincidence.

At the time of this career change, coaching was pretty much unheard of. I hired a coach to make sure this profession was the right fit. As with so many things in life, when you become the student, you have the opportunity to learn about yourself. The shifts I experienced while working with my coach were eye-opening, to say the least. I was setting goals such as going for monthly massages (rare back then and reserved mostly for people with medical issues), doing regular walks in nature (equally as foreign, especially with a long commute to work), and reading self-development books (what are those?), all the while with a newborn baby. I was sold on this industry after witnessing firsthand the impact it had on me personally.

I got certified right away and started taking clients while working at my insurance job, with one of my very first clients driving an hour to meet me to do our sessions via nature walks. The process itself became such a catalyst for my overall happiness that I wanted to share the experience with my clients.

And what I learned about self-care (and about myself) was this: I was nicer to be around because I was *happier*. This in turn rippled outward to everyone in my life—my husband, my son, my family, my friends, and later, my clients. My stress started melting away and was replaced with joy and inspiration. I had more patience. I didn't realize exactly what it was at the time, but I essentially had more love and joy to give. *And* I actually started enjoying my insurance job again, even though I knew I still wanted to pursue coaching. I became a nicer, more giving person at my job, sharing the latest on the personal development books I was reading and even calling my assistant by her first name and thanking her for her help—which she shared that no one in the office had ever done either! *What the...*

This realization is the biggie: self-care is *not* self-ish. Repeat after me. Self-care is not self-ish. Self-care is pretty much as important as breathing. Yep, I just said that. It's truly *that* important. Important in terms of the life we're living, important in terms of being able to stand at the solid centre of our overall well-being and happiness, important in terms of what we are cocreating with the universe for both ourselves and those around us, and important in terms of living the life we've imagined for ourselves. I'd say it's pretty worthy of being taken seriously.

What I've since recognized is that there is a direct correlation between how we take care of ourselves and what we're creating in our lives. Because happiness, peace, and calm, as I've mentioned, extend outward. Think about when you've had a bad day. Not a coincidence that things continued to spiral downwards. And the same for when we're happy. Not a coincidence that things seem to just *flow* on those days.

Our decisions, as we've learned, all stem back to our subconscious mind and our belief systems. Let's do a little exercise to demonstrate this on a personal level. Take a deep, grounding breath, and close your eyes. Think of a time when you were on top of the world. When everything was *flowing up* and your life felt balanced and amazing. Once you have that memory in your mind, notice what you were doing. How were you feeling? What was possible from this place? What was your decision-making process like from there?

Open your eyes and look around. Now close them again, and think of a time when things *weren't* going well. When you were feeling off and a little down and out. Nothing you were doing seemed to be working, and you felt like something had to give. Once you have that memory in your mind, notice what you were doing. How were you feeling? What did your future look like from this place? What was your decision-making process from this place? Go ahead and open your eyes.

Your decisions were completely different during those two experiences, right? I don't want to leave you hanging though. Close your eyes and go back to the first memory, when things were going well. Feel all the emotions that went with it. Good job. Go ahead and open your eyes. You can see now that the mindset we operate from directly impacts how we make decisions. Likewise, we want to make empowered decisions because that is how we will create empowered (and different) results. By leaning in and applying all the levels of self-care we're going to identify together, you will take yourself there. The intention is to be more empowered, more deeply grounded, and more confident. When we take time for ourselves, we are in essence taking a stand for ourselves and our overall well *be*-ing.

When we take this stand, something beautiful starts to happen—a well-orchestrated chain of events ignites. When we give more to ourselves, we have more to give every single person in our lives. We want to share the love we're feeling. We want to connect and extend this love out to other people. We can't not.

Therefore, self-care is not only not being self-*ish* but it actually leads to becoming self-*less*. You are more generous and kind. You get out of your own way and are operating at the highest vibration, the vibration of love. It's like a mist of love that just showers over everyone it touches. It's happiness that can't help *but* expand. And from a business perspective? You're taking out the *getting* and adding in *serving* at the highest level, which can, without a doubt, be felt by every client and colleague you touch. You are filled up, and you are the most helpful and thoughtful version of yourself you can possibly be, regardless of any business goals and dreams. Because at the end of the day, the primary intention of the business you're in is to help other people. And when you operate from this place, your own dreams just flow.

A client I worked with a few years back was really struggling. She was working at a gym, going to school, *and* trying to run a business as a personal trainer. She was stressed out and overwhelmed, and it wasn't a coincidence that her business had stagnated as a result. During one of our sessions as the weekend was approaching, she had a to-do list a mile long. She was ready to roll up her sleeves and make it a working weekend, even though she was already exhausted and approaching burnout.

I suggested, rather firmly (I can be quite firm when I see the subconscious mind trying to railroad our happiness), that she do something *relaxing* for herself instead. This was after we had identified the limiting belief pattern that was keeping her on the proverbial hamster wheel during a past session. The belief being "I am not enough. People leave me and don't love me." This belief kept her in a place of constantly reaching, constantly trying to achieve, and constantly *doing* to gain that love and approval she so desperately desired. She knew deep down she had to remove herself from this hamster wheel for *herself*. And that if she truly wanted to create different results, she had to do things differently.

Kudos to her—she did it, even though it was uncomfortable. Neither one of us could have predicted the result that would follow. Instead of working and staying inside that weekend, she opted for a long hike with her dogs and left her phone at home. After a few glorious hours in nature, she felt lighter, happier, and more grounded and connected. Lo and behold, she came home to an email from a new client wanting to work with her. She'd attracted this person to her because she'd changed her state of mind, shifted her energy, and *upped* her vibration. This was after being stuck for *months*. You just can't make this stuff up, and it's why I love the power of the universe so much. You can also bet that she had way more to give to this new client after filling her own cup.

Let's start off small with self-care. Think about all the things you enjoy doing, the things that help you feel more peaceful and relaxed. When I've run self-care challenges in the past, sometimes it's just a matter of people allowing themselves to drink their coffee hot! Let's start wherever you are.

What is one thing you can start doing this week (or this month, if putting yourself in the here and now of an entire week feels too overwhelming) that is just for you? Maybe it's taking a long, hot bath; going for a walk; listening to a podcast; playing music; or reading a good book. I want to emphasize there is no wrong way to do this. It's about what makes you—and *only* you—feel good. It's about shifting your state of mind to a more empowered way of *be*-ing, and this will be different for everyone. There is no one size fits all, and be wary of anyone who might tell you that you have to do it this way or that way. Those are just things that have worked for *them*; they may or may not work for you. Remember: it comes back to your thoughts and feelings. Any *shoulds* or *have-tos* or *musts* will defeat (and deflate) the entire purpose. Give yourself full permission to do whatever is most comfortable for you.

If you're new to all this, set one or two goals for the month. If you've been practicing for a while, add to what you're doing with the intention of getting to the place of doing something for yourself on the daily. Like anything, if it's not on the calendar, we won't do it. Get out your schedule right now—I know your phone is nearby—and schedule when you can start. Do it right now. I love making my *personal time* in my Google Calendar an inspiring colour—yep, you guessed it! It's blue. Treat this time with the utmost importance and respect, just as you would a business meeting, and rest assured this act of allowing yourself to *receive* will go a long way with the universe. We will discuss this in detail later, with the intention of building a solid self-care practice as we go.

Begin to pay attention to what time in your day works best for you as well. Years ago I realized I was rushing to get to the end of my day so I could have a little time to myself, and my own coach at the time suggested I carve out time in the morning instead. I shifted my me time to the mornings instead, and this made *all* the difference, especially when my kids were little. I was being proactive with starting my day already being filled up instead of reacting to a busy day with one more thing to fit in. They are teenagers now, and this remains my coveted time. Seek—and you shall find—*your* coveted time too. Make it a priority.

One of my clients was able to build a six-figure coaching business once she began practicing copious amounts of self-care. She even joked, "Is this really okay? To practice all this self-care?" The results didn't lie, though, and it turned out it was *more* than okay. Remember: what we put out comes back—*always*.

On that note, let's chat a little bit about these *universal laws* so that we have an understanding on what is happening energetically when we practice self-care. There are many laws of the universe, but *the law of attraction*, *the law of vibration*, and *the law of cause and effect* are the most powerful in my experience. Let's look at these three together.

The law of attraction is the one the movie *The Secret* so brilliantly introduced to the world, and it's what ignited my spiritual journey after losing a loved one unexpectedly. I'll never forget where I was when my world came crashing down. I was on maternity leave. (Don't hate us, but in Canada, moms get twelve months off for maternity leave!) I was just starting month two with my first child, and I was so excited to be having friends over, one with her first child, also a newborn, and the other pregnant with her first child. *Plus* they were bringing me a Tim

Hortons coffee! (If you know Canada, you know there is a Tim Hortons on every corner.)

Well, all of a sudden, my mom showed up at the door, acting really weird. Shortly after that, my husband came home from work—this was all in the *morning*. Something was completely wrong. He told me he needed to talk to me, so I followed him into the bedroom. He immediately broke down into tears and told me it was my dad. And in that moment, I knew. My heart told me before my husband even got the words out. The most awful thing had happened. Somehow I'd known, deep down, for most of my life, that it was going to happen. From the age of nine, I'd known. I even shared this with a psychologist I'd seen to help me navigate my dad's alcohol addiction, who completely brushed it off, telling me alcoholics live well into their seventies. The news I knew was coming for years came. My dad had died.

I entered my spiritual journey kicking and screaming. I was overcome with grief and experiencing sadness on such a profound level. My dad was one of my most favourite people. He was fun, loving, and boy, was he funny. We had the best time together while I was growing up. This was a loss that would shake me to my core. With being an only child and my parents divorcing when I was little, I also felt completely alone in the months that followed. Even though family members tried to help, there was only so much they could do. And only one friend had experienced any kind of loss like that at that time in our lives, so it was hard for any of my friends to relate. (If I can give any advice on this, if you're not sure what to do or say when the loved one of someone you know passes, *always* say or do something. Any acknowledgement helps tremendously.)

About seven months later, I went out to lunch with a girl-friend and was finally beginning to feel better. We had the best time sitting in the sunshine on a patio. Spring is a big deal in Ontario, Canada, especially after the long winters. When I got home that day, I thought, "I'm going to watch that movie *The Secret*." My mom had given me a copy (thank you, Mom!), which had been sitting in my house untouched for a month. I always think it's funny that it took being in a good mood to finally watch the movie, which is what the movie is all about. Like attracts like.

The law of attraction states that we are all energy and that like attracts like—similar energy attracts similar energy—even if we aren't consciously aware of it. Our thoughts create our feelings, and it's the feelings that put out the energy. This is where the subconscious mind comes into play. It's the feelings we are operating from deep down that are dictating what we are creating. Therefore, we are always *attracting* positivity or negativity based on the energy (feeling) we are putting out. And it's actually not even so much that we're attracting it to us. This tripped me up for years. Thinking that what we want is in some faraway place and that we attract it to ourselves. In reality, it's already there for us, but we literally don't see it when we aren't operating at the same frequency of energy. This is why so many people don't think it works.

Here's an example: I was feeling off in my business for a few months at one point. Nothing seemed to be flowing, and I entered what I like to call a *doubt spiral*. I was doubting everything and thinking about quitting. I really wanted to do more speaking engagements, and I kept thinking to check my inbox, but I would talk myself out of it because I knew there weren't any new emails. Every few weeks I would *think* about checking it but wouldn't, my own doubt holding me back.

I finally started feeling better. Even though I felt off, I really wanted to feel better and figure this stuff out. A little willingness goes a long way. Through the deeper belief work we've been talking about, I finally felt better because I raised my own vibration. And the next time I thought to check my inbox, *I did it*. I acted on my thoughts and made the deliberate decision of checking my inbox.

Lo and behold, buried deep down in a string of emails from months back was an email from a lady I had met at a networking event asking me to speak to her community of entrepreneurs. And this led to not one but *six* speaking engagements! You can see the power of the subconscious mind at work here. I had been seeing through a lens of doubt and anxiety. It wasn't until I shifted my state of mind, both conscious and subconscious, that I was able to see the opportunity that was there, waiting for me the whole time. This is how the law of attraction works. The way to create what we're wanting is there for us the entire time; we just don't always notice it.

The law of vibration is very similar to the law of attraction in that it refers to us being energy. It takes the concept a little further and implies that every living thing vibrates at a certain frequency. It's basically an extension of the law of attraction but helps us see how important the energy in which we are vibrating at is. For our purposes this pertains to our thoughts. Our thoughts and feelings vibrate at a certain frequency, and to create more of what we want in our lives, we need to vibrate on the frequency of what we're wanting. This is what is behind the concept of what we put out comes back and why self-care is a major part of the equation. We want to be vibrating at the same level as what we are wanting more of in our lives (i.e., peace, calm, love, and abundance) and operate less on the level of what we don't want (i.e., overwhelm, anxiety, fear, and doubt). Through belief work, we can identify what frequency we've actually been operating on and consciously change it.

The law of cause and effect states that for every single action in the universe, there is a reaction. For every effect in the world, there is a cause. Just think about anything in life, any action you take. There is always a consequence or reaction for anything we do. The real kicker, though, and for our purposes, is that the *cause* is always our thinking, which most people don't realize. It's our thinking, and therefore the subsequent *feeling* that we put out that creates what is showing up in our external world (the effect). It always comes back to our thoughts and the energy around them. If something isn't going the way you want, you must take a deeper look at the thoughts responsible for the outcome. This newfound responsibility is humbling but also liberating.

If you emit a stressed-out, anxiety-filled energy, it's not a coincidence that you will get exactly that back. You might be stressing about where the next client is coming from (low vibration), and then your washing machine breaks down (equally low vibration), both of which create even higher cumulative stress levels, especially if money is tight.

Here's a guarantee: the effect of the cause will show up somewhere, somehow, at some time in your life or business. It's like a boomerang: what you throw out there won't just stay out there; it will return. The universe doesn't just stay in one lane either, and this is why I always say if one area of your life is off, it's likely impacting another area, such as your business. Often, entrepreneurial business problems have nothing to do with the business itself, and I can't tell you how often forgiveness work is needed for someone to get unstuck in their business. (More on forgiveness in an upcoming chapter.)

The great news is that this law of cause and effect also applies to a happy, relaxed energy. If we take the time to do what we love, shift our perspective from fear to love, we become happier and more relaxed, and like the *chain reaction* I described earlier, we begin to *show up* happier and more relaxed as well. Like a spring shower, this happy, relaxed energy showers down to those around us, and this is when good things begin to happen, such as more clients to serve or the opportunity to change lives with a speaking engagement. And this is *all* because we have changed the vibrational state we are operating from (the cause) and creating amazing things in our lives (the effect).

Are there lessons to learn? Absolutely. And that goes back to the belief work, which we will be revisiting over and over throughout this book. We can't just *will* ourselves into positive thoughts or cover them up with a spiritual Band-Aid. Keep gaining awareness around the beliefs keeping you where you are and making the decisions you do, like we identified in chapter 1.

Strategically, what happens is that we become more resourceful when we practice self-care. We have created the time and space to receive the universal guidance that is there for all of us. We cannot receive this energy and this guidance with a cluttered mind. In essence, we become more resourceful because we've levelled the playing field and created more room in our lives for loving energy. This allows us to rise to the same energetic level as the solution, and before we know it, we have elevated manifesting status. We cannot see the solutions from the level of the problem. Remember the speaking engagements I told you about earlier. I had to shift my state to receive the solution.

I will say this though: it takes practice. It's like going to the gym—we cannot and should not stop after achieving the desired results. No. We keep going because we're so happy with what we've created that we want to *continue*. It's the same with self-care. We've had a lot of years of programming and conditioning around hustling. To constantly achieve and take on more based on our misplaced beliefs. It's not that having goals and dreams is bad; it's the way we go about achieving them that can so often lead to downward spirals, if we're not careful and cognizant. When we operate from fear and *not enoughness*, for instance, we maintain a hustle mentality. When we operate from a place of self-acceptance, however, we slow ourselves down and *expand*.

But beware—practicing self-care with deliberate intention will become addictive. Why? Because doing what we love feels *good*. It feels so good that you will want to do it more and more. Happiness catches—and spreads—like wildfire. After a while, you might even begin to feel *off* when you *don't* do it. I got to a point where my daily morning routine just wasn't enough. Walks with the dog and hot baths in the evenings also became my saving grace.

What I also realized is that some days I just wake up feeling off—it still happens sometimes—and on those off days, I'm always tempted to let my morning self-care practice go. To hop on my phone and look at social media or the news. And I decided years ago not to look at the news, as I just felt it was predominantly fear-based. But in keeping with the whole *like attracts like*, it's not a coincidence I tend to choose something of a fear-based nature when I feel off. But when I force myself to do my morning routine anyway, which helps ground and balance me, guess what happens? I feel better, of course! Any worries or anxieties that were plaguing me are quickly put into perspective, and I can see they don't actually matter much, or at least the heavier thoughts around them fall away. We have to make ourselves do what feels good!

Over the years I have also come to realize that self-care isn't just about taking the time to do a self-care practice, although that's important. It's more of a way of *be*-ing. Getting to the place of asking ourselves throughout the day, week, month, and year, "What do I *need* in this moment?" Because old patterns die hard, and the more awareness we have around this, the freer and more peaceful we will be. But don't stress. We don't need to figure all that out now; just know this way of *be*-ing is coming, and it is where we will shift to by the end of our time together.

It's not a coincidence that my biggest creations, along with my worst manifestations, come directly from my state of mind. And I can say with 100 percent certainty that everything you are wanting to manifest comes back to this foundation.

COACH APPROACH

With every change we make, we must tune in to the supporting beliefs that have to go alongside them. This is why change doesn't always stick. We have to be willing to not only *do* something new but to *change* our beliefs as well; remember, per the law of cause and effect, addressing the root cause. To really give yourself permission to do what you love in *all* areas of life, you need to have an empowered, enduring belief system to support your endeavours. In the previous chapter, we discovered the disempowered belief keeping you where you are, and now we will determine the *new* way of thinking, along with the action steps, that will help you create your empowered future instead.

Get your notebook and pen. Move into the neutral spot on the floor that we mapped out in the previous chapter, and again move yourself physically into that spot. From this neutral place, look at the empowered future you mapped out before on the ground, where everything you want to create has already happened. Do not step into this spot yet; just *look* at it and think about what that type of a future *looks like* for you. Get a clear picture of it in your mind. Good job.

Moving forward, every time you step into the empowered future spot on the ground, you are going to act like you've already achieved it. So when you physically step into that space, you have already created everything you're wanting there. Go ahead and step into the empowered future spot now. Remember to bring your pen and paper to this new spot. Now ask yourself the following questions, and write them down in your notebook while you're standing in this spot:

1. What is it like here? How does it feel? Think about all the feelings coming up in this place. Has your heart rate mellowed? Have your breathing patterns changed? What physical manifestations are occurring? Where do you feel them in your body? What is possible from this place? Write it all down. Good job!

2. Step back into the neutral spot on the floor, and take a few deep, cleansing breaths. While looking at the empowered space, tune in and ask yourself what is the main belief you need to have to create this empowered life for yourself? What do you need to believe? It might be the opposite of the disempowered belief you identified in chapter 1, or it might be a little different. Remember: there is no right or wrong answer. Write it all down.

3. Step back into the empowered spot on the ground while fully embracing this new belief. Good job.

4. Now ask yourself what you needed to change, shift, or let go of to have this future. Sometimes it's helpful to look over your shoulder to truly think about what it took to get here and what needed to change or be done differently. What thoughts did you need to have? What steps did you take? What actions did you make? Get as specific as possible. For example, if it was positive thoughts that helped, what did you do daily to generate these positive thoughts? Did you meditate? Read uplifting books? Go to a yoga class? Write down everything you just mapped out as to how you made this future lifestyle happen.

5. Now think about the positive intention you identified in chapter 1 that kept you in the disempowered place. How is it honoured here, in this empowered future and way of being? Good job. Write that down too.

6. In this empowered space, think about everything you just identified. Fully realize what it is like here, where you have achieved this amazing lifestyle and business *already*, while fully embracing this new and empowered belief about yourself. Notice how your physiology, your thoughts,

and the impact on the different areas of your life, such as relationships, health, finances, and work, are different here.

7. Repeat your new, empowered belief, and think about everything you did to get here. Notice how it feels all through your body. What is one word that describes how you're feeling in this moment? Go with whatever word pops up. Maybe even write that word down. Take a few deep, cleansing breaths to embody the feelings associated with the word you chose while repeating the word. Awesome! You can come out of this space anytime!

You've actually accomplished several important things here. First, you anchored yourself in the empowered state of mind on that specific spot on the floor. You can stand in it anytime to shift your state. It's a great place to both strengthen and revisit. Second, you anchored in those feelings with a single identifying *word*. As you strengthen that state by standing in that spot on the ground repeating the word you chose, you will also get to the place of just *thinking* about the word and invoking those feelings. It is so powerful. (My word was *bliss*, and to this day, it invokes the exact feeling I felt when I was standing in my empowered space on the ground: instant *bliss*.)

Remember that the word you choose should reflect the emotion you're really wanting to create that goes along with your empowered lifestyle, and the more we can strengthen this state, the more you will operate from it. Spend time in your empowered space as often as you can to really strengthen this new way of operating. Affirm your word repeatedly outside your space too; whether it's having the word appear as your screen saver, writing the word on a sticky note, or jotting it down on a pad on your nightstand. Use your imagination, and like anything you want to stick, carve out some space in your calendar for when it suits you to spend time in this space. By having the word in front of you often—and I suggest writing down the empowered belief you identified as well—it will help you stay focused on this feeling and empowered belief throughout your day. Decide now what tool you would like to use to have the word and belief in front of you.

Congratulations! You have also taken the first steps towards creating an inspired action plan. In step four, you tuned inward to discover the path that will enable you to achieve your empowered future. Everything that you wrote down is your unique road map. How cool is that? And what I love about this exercise, out of the hundreds of people I've taken through, all (I literally can't think of one person who didn't) mapped out some kind of self-care plan as the way to get there. Whether it was through thinking of positive thoughts or taking care of themselves. We seem to intuitively know this is the way to reach our goals in an inspired way. The self-care activities you identified earlier in this chapter were likely enhanced and more clearly defined during this part of the exercise. Go ahead and assign dates to these inspired action steps, and add them to your calendar. Do it now in a way that is manageable and doable for you.

We have done *a lot* of heavy lifting in this chapter. Be proud! You have identified the self-care you want to add to your schedule (with a fun colour to boot), and you have begun to identify the beliefs you need to have to create your empowered future. You've also begun to understand and absorb how all this *feels* and the inspired action steps that will take you there. You are taking a stand for *you* and putting *you* back into your life and business.

You're probably already feeling lighter and more empowered. Yay! Be prepared for this to continue, and be strengthened. Let's set the intention that this next leg of your business growth will be more firmly led by and aligned with these universal laws, where you allow the universe to cocreate with you. Remember: you don't have to do it alone.

The process of making more room for these universal laws to manifest in your own life should be deliberate and purposeful. In fact, the act of *making room*, *clearing the clutter*, and creating space for new growth is what we will explore in the next chapter.

3

CLEAR OUT
THE CLUTTER

Creating Space for Growth

IMAGINE TRYING TO FORCE-FIT ONE more thing into your junk drawer, only to find it's completely full and absolutely cannot fit one more thing. You're now faced with a choice: keep expending energy trying to cram in more junk, or take the time to clean it out and create an organized, functional space.

It's the same with your mind. Even though you added in a few self-care activities in chapter 2 that helped you find your footing and gain momentum, you won't be able to fully take on more (especially new and inspired work projects) if you're at max capacity (a result of old, disempowered decisions). This applies to both your physical and mental environments, with thoughts and emotions being even more cumbersome than a cluttered physical environment. A fairly recent study shows we have around 6,200 thoughts per day. That's a lot of thoughts! If we don't consciously fill our minds with what we want, as we've learned in the preceding chapters, our minds will do it for us.

Our thoughts are directly connected to what is going on in both our physical and emotional environments. It's all connected. Every time we even *think* about something happening in our life or in our business that we need to get done, it plays on in our minds and takes up time and energy.

Consider this example: Say your car needs repairing. If you continue to think, "I have to get the car fixed," it will continue to stay on your mind until you get it done. We tend to think about these things and then don't do anything about them for a while since they don't seem to be pressing. We continue to repeat the thoughts without taking the action. Every single time we think about it, though, and don't do anything about it it's actually draining our time and energy, thus taking us away from what we really want to be doing. And we have big goals and dreams!

It's those thoughts that continue to pull at us, depleting our energy and creating stress, anxiety, and a feeling of being overwhelmed. Every time we think about something on the to-do list, we are giving our power over to it, allowing our circumstances to control us and how we spend our time instead of the other way around—consciously deciding.

In the first two chapters, we started looking at what is driving the decisions to add more to our plates to begin with, which we will continue to address, but we must clear out the old clutter from past decisions in the meantime, in both our physical and mental environments. And let's be honest, there are always going to be things that we need to get done, tasks that need tending to, especially with running a household and a business simultaneously, but we can start to lighten the load a little bit and be more aware of our decisions moving forward.

We want to start off by looking at everything we are tolerating in our lives. In the coaching world, we call them *tolerations*. A toleration is essentially anything you put up with, or *tolerate*, in your life. It could be living in a less-than-desirable place, being in a toxic relationship, or driving around in a messy car. Anything goes. And every single time we *think* about these tolerations (without doing anything about them, that is), they distract us from proactively being happy and doing more of what we love.

When I first started coaching professionally and before I discovered my niche, I was working with several professional women who wanted to discover their purpose. They were so overwhelmed with life that we started with the all-important task of *clearing out the clutter* first to have the time and energy to even enable them to connect with their deepest desires. As we've learned, we cannot hear the universal guidance if we don't create the space. Our thoughts about the never-ending to-do list are loud, noisy, and downright boisterous. They keep us tightly wrapped in a cocoon of misery. So we need to address where the noise is coming from.

What happened with these ladies? When they cleared out the clutter, something wonderful *naturally* started to happen. They had more space to do the things they loved. They brought the joy back into their lives. And lo and behold, they *both* started their own businesses and left the corporate world! And not that this is the path for everyone, but they created the space to not only connect with but also follow their deepest dreams. Dreams that had been silenced and thus rendered inactive because of all the noise.

Let's go ahead and tackle your tolerations in the four main areas of life: *physical environment, emotional well-being, finances,* and *health*, with a sprinkle of *spirituality* as a bonus fifth area. Roll up your sleeves, grab your notebook, and let's dive in! If you're listening to the audio version of this book or are somewhere where you can't write things down, then stop, schedule thirty minutes on your calendar to revisit, and come back to this then.

We're going to start with your *physical* landscape because quite frankly, it's the easiest to identify.

For my husband, it's *always* the garage. Our garage is the bottomless pit, the endless dumping ground for everyone in our family. When we clean up inside the house, what we purge usually goes in the garage—probably partially because we don't have basements in Southern California—and it drives my husband bonkers. Every so often, probably once a quarter, we thoroughly clean and reorganize the garage. He can't relax with a messy garage, and I love the manifesting that accompanies the power of this cleanout! It never fails; whatever we are working on creating in our lives always seems to show up after we purge the garage. Is the universe watching us? No. But it surely *feels* us.

Remember: what we put out comes back to us. Stress breeds stress. Peace creates peace. The phrase "nature abhors a vacuum," which is attributed to Aristotle, states that every space in nature needs to be filled with something. And with our knowledge of the universal laws, it's going to get filled with what we put out. It's not a coincidence that the path to what we're wanting to create becomes visible as a result of a good clearout. We see the next steps because we've cleared out the mental thoughts associated with the physical clutter in our lives.

Go ahead and take inventory of the physical spaces that are a part of your life. Whether it's your office, home, car, or even a second home. All spaces that are a part of your life count because they *all* have the ability to eat up your time and energy. Set a timer on your cell phone for five minutes, then write down all the things that are currently bothering you in those environments, the things that are creating clutter in your mind and taking up space. Some examples are disorganized papers in your office, old clothes that no longer fit, a messy playroom, crumbs in the cutlery drawer (how does that even happen?), a never-ending supply of serving platters (this is where I started—why do we need so many *platters*?), a washing machine that needs repairing—the list goes on and on.

It's also important to look at any physical objects you are holding on to out of obligation. For example, china that has been passed down that you don't love. *It's okay to let it go.* This is your home and space. This was something that was important to *someone else*, not to you. Maybe you can donate the china (or whatever the item in question) or give it away to someone who does love it and make their day. We are going to learn how to be *proactive* with saying no in the next chapter. For now, though, ask yourself the question, "What am I keeping out of obligation?" Just add those things to your list. You don't have to take any drastic action right now. Simply make your list.

Along the same wavelength, is there anything in your physical environment that is causing you sadness or another heavier emotion? An example could be a portrait of a loved one who has passed. If it's creating a heaviness or if it's reviving your grief every time you look at it, then let's put it away for awhile. Of course, we want to honour and memorialize those we have lost, but maybe there is a different way of accomplishing that goal that doesn't bring sadness to you daily. Or maybe more healing needs to be done to get to the place where seeing a photo or a portrait of a passed loved one isn't debilitating and painful.

Once you have completed your list, we're going to move on to the next area of your life: your *emotional* well-being. As you have already seen, it's the thoughts we have that keep us in a place of disdain and disorder. We want to examine what exactly is triggering those heavier thoughts. We examined belief systems in the last two chapters and now have an understanding of where our decisions come from. Now we want to identify what exactly triggers this disempowered way of being. What are the thoughts that are pulling you over to that disempowered space, preventing you from living a more empowered life?

This example will really hit home: I had just been appointed as a new board member for a philanthropic nonprofit right when the annual fundraiser was about to begin, which I somehow agreed to spearhead. The micromanaging that ensued by the person in charge was, quite frankly, unbearable. I'm talking nitpicking to the *n*th degree. And even though I could see it for what it was, it didn't mean it didn't impact me. It awakened my core wound of not being good enough, a.k.a. not a good enough person, and these feelings were being triggered left, right, and centre. Every time this person would nitpick, it triggered something deep within me. It became utterly exhausting in just a short period of time. After some honest, open discussions with both my husband and a very good friend, I realized my core wound was being triggered. Therein lay my lesson. To remember and affirm, "I am good enough, and I've done nothing wrong. I am a good person." I later learned I wasn't alone in this, with other people being at their wits' end with this person as well. Something had to shift.

I then asked the universe for help, as I didn't want to quit after just joining, but I knew it wasn't worth the energy that I was expending. It's situations like these where the term *energy vampire* comes into play. Well, lo and behold, this person's situation changed, and it no longer made sense for them to serve on the board. The universe *took care* of it for me. This isn't to imply we shouldn't stick up for ourselves; a more senior board member did step in to have a conversation with this person before the ultimate solution presented itself. The solution the universe presented ended up being the best for everyone involved, including the one instigating the excess stress. As it turned out, this person was stressed out and overwhelmed and also navigating issues with extreme perfectionism. This story is a great example for all of us to also see what it's like to be on the receiving end of such perfectionism, myself included.

This example shows us how the emotional situations with others can play on our minds. These situations are mentally, physically, and emotionally exhausting, to say the least. But they present us with an opportunity to grow, to look at our own triggers, and at a certain point, they teach us valuable lessons about self-love and about who (and what) we allow into our space. Even though I truly believe we are all connected and a part of something bigger at our highest level, it doesn't mean we should act as a doormat in the meantime. That is not a loving vibration. Taking a stand for how we spend our time and energy is empowering *and* within our control. We always have a choice.

Go ahead and take inventory of your emotional landscape. Again, set the timer for five minutes, and list everything that is irritating you, saddening you, angering you, and so on. Identify all those heavier emotions. Here we are going to refrain from listing any to-dos that need to get done, even though they could be causing stress. The to-do list falls more under the other sections. This section is about the emotional heaviness you are carrying around and the need to clear out the clutter that those heavy emotions can create. Just see what comes up when you are looking primarily at your emotions. Some examples are a conflict with a colleague, a client not respecting boundaries, a family member not using your entrepreneurial services (this is a big one, mompreneurs!), or a spouse not *hearing* you. This section tends to involve other people but could be inwardly focused too. Inward examples are beating yourself up about failing to reach a certain goal or the guilt arising out of not spending enough time with your kids, extended family, friends, or even yourself.

Sidebar: For those of you who wrote down your spouse, I want to take this opportunity to address unsupportive spouses (or life partners). This has come up time and time again with my coaching clients, which honestly makes sense. Usually, one person in the relationship is attracted to personal development work first. That person becomes filled with excitement and unbridled enthusiasm about the possibility of there being another way to live life. The other partner is often less than thrilled with this new turn of events, this dramatic new way of thinking. When we think about the subconscious mind, it tracks. The less-than-thrilled partner feels safe and cosy where they are, and this type of *change* feels anything but safe. The best advice I can give here is to have an honest conversation with your partner about what it is that attracts you to learning and growing and what this means for you and your bigger family picture. If your partner is open to learning and growing, too, then that's really all you can ask for. They might not be at the same speed as you, or they might even breeze on by you!

My husband and I used to have the biggest philosophical debates, and several times I wasn't sure we were going to make it. He came into our relationship with a more extensive knowledge about philosophy than I did, and he *always* made a great argument. After I preached for years the principles of the law of attraction, he didn't fully get on board until we attended a seminar on the specifics of the subconscious mind. He was all in after that, with even travelling with me to faraway places for mastermind meetings and participating in coaching. We went through a lot of deep self-exploration—together—during that time.

And who am I kidding? We continue to debate these topics at even deeper depths the more we both grow and evolve. It's what keeps us spicy! All I can say is the speed at which this growth occurs really isn't up to us, but having love and compassion is. One that I'm still learning and practicing as I continue to seek new depths of my personal and spiritual development.

Let's go ahead and move on. You are ready. Apart from my sidebar above, we are not offering up a solution or what to do next right now. We are just taking inventory and becoming *aware*.

Our next section is our *finances*. This is a biggie. There is a lot of stress and anxiety tied to our financial security, and because of this, it gets (and deserves) its own section.

What I've noticed in myself over the years is that anytime my core wound of *not enoughness* got triggered, it would *immediately* carry over to money. I would start worrying about it even when there was nothing to worry about. It's fascinating when we start becoming aware of these emotions and thought patterns. It's like the core wound gets triggered, and once that wound is reopened and awakened, it automatically looks for *close cousins* to support it—that is, other debilitating emotions, such as fear, worry, and doubt. All these patterns and all these destructive emotions stem from our subconscious mind. Like we talked about in chapter 1, we want to bring these thoughts and stories to our conscious awareness. Although that type of worrying can still take place from time to time, it becomes less frequent, and with regular practice and by setting an empowered intention, we can shift these heavier, judgemental thoughts faster. To me, this is the true purpose of personal development work—not removing these debilitating thoughts altogether but seeing how *quickly* we can shift them.

Let's try this. Again, set your timer for five minutes, and make a list of everything you are tolerating around money and finances. Some examples are not having a savings account or retirement plan set up, not paying yourself first, not having enough to cover your monthly needs (not wants but *needs*), not allowing yourself to have fun, the list goes on and on, and you know your own unique list better than anyone. I should state here that I am not a financial planner by any means. The purpose of this exercise is merely to become *aware* of what is draining your time and energy from a financial perspective.

After taking a deep dive into these concepts and running one of my money makeover retreats, what happened to one of the attendees was nothing short of miraculous. First, she had her spouse do the exercises afterwards. They put themselves on the same page by starting a budget and looking at their expenditures while examining their individual beliefs about money. They started making changes about how they were approaching their finances as a result. She had also been working on up-levelling her clientele. As a real estate agent, she wanted to attract relationships with buyers and sellers who were in the $2 million home bracket.

Well, during the retreat, she realized she actually harboured some pretty ill feelings towards *those* people with money, some pretty harsh assumptions, such as they are selfish and don't value anyone else. Ouch, right? But she's not alone. Many of us have or have had some variation of those feelings and emotions unfortunately, due to the programming we grew up with, whether it was verbally shared or just the overall *vibe* we picked up from those around us. And because we don't want to *be* that type of person (selfish and not valuing others), it creates a value conflict deep down, and we end up holding ourselves back from growing our businesses *subconsciously*.

What happened next was incredible: Because of the heightened awareness she experienced and because of her ability to shift her subconscious thought patterns to a more positive place, she closed a sale on a house that was becoming impossible to sell, with her client pulling out of escrow twice and letting his fear cause a bunch of issues. She also attracted a major investor as a client, who was in the $4 *million range*! And as if that wasn't enough, she also attracted a new listing (a seller) when she had been primarily attracting buyers and already had multiple offers within a couple of days!

And just like that, things *shifted* for her.

I'm happy to report that at the time of writing this book, she just closed on a $6.2 million house! All because she followed the principles we are addressing in this book.

It's amazing what happens when we start to gain control over this process. Even making just the smallest shift, such as organizing your bank accounts and paying attention to what you are spending, sends out a powerful, purposeful energy to the universe. You are taking a stand for yourself by getting organized and are essentially saying you can handle more. From an energetic perspective, you are putting out feelings of empowerment, which, again, always come back.

Let's now look at *health*. I was hesitant to include this one, as there is so much emphasis (or *over*emphasis, I should say) in our culture right now about looking perfect and being at the perfect weight, but there is much to be said about looking at what we are tolerating when it comes to our health. Without our health, it's hard to create much else. This isn't about being at our perfect weight. It's about being proactive about our overall health and energy. This could look like going to the dentist regularly, having our eyes checked, exercising, and eating well.

One exercise I still use from my Coach University days, where I was initially certified as a life coach, is something called the "clean sweep." It has us take a full inventory of these four main areas of life. In the health area, it asks if we floss every day. This one has always resonated with me. How many of us do the walk of shame out of the dentist's office after receiving a thorough talking-to about not flossing? We know it's good for us, but we still don't do it. Well, somewhere along the way, after realizing I talk so much about self-care but was still *too busy* to floss, I decided, "Gosh, darn it, I'm worth it!" (Insert the *Saturday Night Live* character Stuart Smalley's voice here.) I started taking more time for myself with getting ready for the day and taking care of my body—*and* my teeth! It felt amazing. Making time for those simple acts of *self-love*.

Let's look at what you are *tolerating*. Set the timer for five minutes, and write down everything you are tolerating health-wise. This also can pertain to mental health. Maybe there is something you are tolerating in your life that is making you feel off. This is an example of where these areas can overlap. If anything causing heavier feelings wasn't already included in another area, be sure to include it here.

It's not uncommon for mompreneurs to naturally start evaluating their health. When we clean up all the other areas, this is a natural extension. As business starts flowing, we clean up more and more areas, and even newer depths are then reached resultswise. One of my clients became so in tune with her body as a result of all this personal development work that when she found out she had a cyst that could have become a potential issue, she healed it herself through her thoughts. I'm not suggesting everyone try that, of course, but it's amazing how far the healing and love can extend when we consciously take the time for ourselves.

And last but not least is our *spirituality*. I am including this area because I know many of you reading this have a desire in your hearts to bring more meaning to your lives. You are wanting to connect with that divine energy that is there for all of us. So let's take a peek at what you've been wanting to do but aren't. What are you judging yourself for not doing? What do you wish you were doing more of?

I once had a client who was a Reiki master. She knew her spiritual practice was important to her but had been neglecting it. Like all things that are good for us, they usually are the first to fall by the wayside, especially when we start feeling good. We somehow think we've got this and let our practices trickle off. She let her morning self-care practice slide, which had been a very intentional practice that included spiritual acts such as meditation. When she added back her morning meditation, she started feeling calmer and more grounded again—and not at all by coincidence; her business results started flowing again too.

It's important to reiterate here again that there is no right or wrong way of having a spiritual/self-love practice. It's whatever makes *you* feel more connected. It could be going for a run or connecting with other people; it's whatever works for you. Meditation is just what worked for this particular person. Again, it's all about shifting the *state* we are operating from, not as much the *how* we go about doing it.

Take five minutes, and jot everything down. Some examples are wanting to meditate, wanting to take more time for yourself, learning more about manifesting, practicing forgiveness—again, you know your list better than anyone.

I have discovered in my own life that the more I continue to let go and become more connected with the universe, every single thing around me flows more freely. I become more connected to higher-level thinking, which allows me to see solutions almost instantaneously. The more I surrender trying to control everything and the more I trust in something bigger than myself, the more I see the beauty in others and also the most amazing opportunities. Psst, what I am able to see through this more expansive lens is *always* far better and brighter than I could ever dream up for myself!

It's this kind of spiritual expansion that led to us to buying a home in our dream area, even though we'd been told many times that this home-buying dream would be impossible for us to attain. It's this kind of positive spiritual opening up that has led to us buying multiple investment properties; this opening up has helped guide our every step and will continue to guide us moving forward. I love every single second of cocreating with the universe. Sometimes even more so than the outcome! And if I can do it, so can you!

Really great job! Be so proud of yourself for making the time to take inventory in all four areas of your life—physical environment, emotional well-being, finances, and health—and our fifth bonus, spirituality. This is no small feat, especially when you're reading this book at the same time. The beauty of pairing these exercises with reading this book is that you are, in effect, giving the book an opportunity to be your road map and your guide as you move forward. It's a lot to move through, and if you weren't able to do it this time around, don't stress. Get out your schedule, add thirty minutes to your calendar, and do it later. But do it!

It's important to mention that this practice of identifying these *tolerations* in your life is not meant to be about striving towards perfection. We are humans, uniquely imperfect and constantly evolving. Perfection should never be our goal. It's not about having your house in perfect order or having the perfect clothes to wear. It *is* about looking at what you are tolerating in your life that is draining your time and energy. I appreciate this is a slippery slope, which is why we must approach this topic with practicality and sensitivity. In fact, we are going to address this toxic topic of perfectionism in depth in a later chapter, but for now, just start to be aware of how it's impacting your decisions as we go. Remember: *self-love starts with awareness.*

For those of you who completed the inventory, you're probably feeling a lot lighter from just calling these things out and bringing them to the light. The power of awareness alone is truly amazing. If you are intentional and consistent in your efforts moving forward, you will start to approach things differently and make new decisions as a result.

COACH APPROACH

Now we're going to look at tackling the tolerations you identified. We're going to start by choosing five tolerations to address, and we can do this in a couple of different ways. You can either choose one from each of the five areas, or if you felt one area stands out over the others, then you may want to start with this section entirely. You can always mix and match too—you can customize this process in a way that feels most authentic and most comfortable to you. Whichever way you choose, try to start with some of the bigger tolerations that, once handled, will actually resolve some of the other smaller ones on the list.

1. Go ahead and choose the five you are going to tackle first. Then assign dates in your calendar to actually *get them done*. If your washing machine needs fixing, for example, you will mark a specific date on your calendar to call a repair person. If your garage needs cleaning, you will put a date (or multiple dates, if needed) on your calendar when you're going to work on it. Note: Be reasonable with what is manageable with your current schedule. You will likely

notice you feel even lighter just by assigning dates. Choose five for now, but continue repeating this process until all your tolerations have been addressed. This will ensure you are consistently taking action. It's also a good idea to take inventory a couple of times throughout the year. We want to be *continually* aware of what is draining our time and energy so that we can address it. You will find that the more you do this, the more you start naturally letting go of clutter and making decisions not to include it from the get-go. Go ahead and make it a recurring item on your calendar, either biannually or annually. Again, you know best what works for you.

2. This is a bonus step to help you shift your thoughts about money. This is one of my favourite exercises to take clients through. *Write a letter to yourself from your money.* Write the letter as if you are your money writing a letter to yourself. Share how it feels about being in a relationship with you. It's pretty eye-opening.

3. Here's another bonus step: Once you've done step 2, think about how you would like to treat your money, and write a letter back to it. *From you to your money.* How will you treat it moving forward? What is important? Then go ahead and pull out one or two *money affirmations* from your letter, and add them to your daily repetition list.

4. Get in the habit of asking the universe to help. I used to love (and still do) asking for a shift in perspective. It never fails to show up, and it *always* helps me see things more clearly and more expansively. Remember that it's subtle shifts like these that bump up your vibration to where the solution lies. These solutions are waiting for you.

5. Continue your self-care activities and action steps from chapter 2 and build on them.
6. Continue to affirm your new belief and empowered word, along with your new money affirmations.

You are probably excited to clear out the clutter! What a powerful shift! Isn't it empowering to take your power back? This is pivotal in *receiving* all the gifts the universe has to offer, which we will continue to open up to moving forward. If you would like to do more of the exercises from the money makeover retreat I mentioned, just visit the resource page I created for you at www.chrisatley.com/resources to access them.

4

IF IT'S NOT AN ABSOLUTE YES, IT'S A NO

Saying No and Setting Boundaries

"I'M GOOD"—THAT'S HOW MY THIRTEEN-YEAR-OLD daughter says no to the things she doesn't want to do. We can't argue with that, right? It's clear *and* respectful. No matter what stage women entrepreneurs are in their growth, it's this beauty I see popping up *all* throughout. Some like to say, "New level, new devil," with regard to reaching new depths in business, but I like to say, "New level, same devil." It's just that core wound in our subconscious popping up again, trying to keep us safe. And saying no to others does not feel safe. At least at first.

There are several things going on in our subconscious mind when it comes to saying no to other people. And let's be clear, in this context, it applies to something you are not keen on doing but are too afraid to refuse, so you do it anyway. We identified in chapter 1 your core limiting belief. It's some form of *not enoughness*, with you believing you are lacking something in some way. Whether you've accepted thoughts about not being good enough, smart enough, safe enough, or even the fear of not being loveable. Deep down, we're afraid of being found out. We do not want to experience the pain of this feeling. And so we stay where we are. Where it feels safe and comfortable. Where we're accustomed to flying under the radar and not ruffling any feathers. Where we say yes when we really want to say no and where we don't say yes *enough* to our own desires and needs. We are the ones making these decisions, though, and are in complete control. Again, it's liberating but also scary at the same time to think about changing this.

At our core we are afraid of the *judgement* we will receive from others. We are afraid of others judging us on whether or not we are good enough or whether or not we are essentially a good person and worthy of love deep down. And we will avoid this feeling like the plague. None of us want to feel like a bad person or unloved, and so we do everything, and I mean everything, to avoid this. We continue making decisions from this disempowered place, not fully living out our true potential. Instead, we fill up our time with *shoulds* and *have-tos*, which place us in situations that are less than optimal. I see this at every single level of entrepreneurship, no matter how much personal development work people have done. The people-pleasing and judgement-avoiding runs thick beneath the surface and has us sticking to it like glue.

We also have to understand that at a deep core, primal level, we simply do not want to be alone. As humans, our primal instinct is to be a part of the group, to belong. It's no secret that people have been kicked out of the group for thinking differently or, in extreme cases, even being killed for having differing beliefs. We have a deep-seated fear of going against the group, and rightly so. No wonder it's so hard to put ourselves out there on social media. We are scared to death—sometimes literally. And remember: even though our conscious mind can reason that we have evolved as a society, the subconscious mind does not have that luxury. As we've learned, all our beliefs in our subconscious mind have been passed down through consistent repetition (society, culture, history, upbringing) and also through any emotional reactions to situations. Society taught us early on that we don't want to be shunned by or expelled from the group, so we stay complacent and trapped in our people-pleasing mode.

I have several painful memories from my adolescent years when I stayed quiet to remain a part of the group. One friend was so vocal in her opinions about everything that I was too afraid to even say I liked the radio station she made fun of for fear of being laughed at and being kicked out of the group. What's interesting is that later on, in high school, when I decided to skip a grade to go to university a year early, this same girl convinced all the other girls in our group to have an *intervention* of sorts, where they ganged up on me at a friend's house.

It was not at all a pleasant experience, but I stood firm on what I was doing—there was that strong will again—and I stayed the course. A few years later, I was blindsided again while having lunch at her house, when she got everyone on board to do the same thing again. (Some nonsense about something I was doing *wrong* in terms of hanging out with the girls in the grade ahead of me.) From that point forward, I began to distance myself from that group. Interestingly, one by one, all the girls in the group saw the truth of this person, and they also left the group.

Even though I ended up not conforming in the end and stayed true to my bigger dreams, those interactions still left a mark. The hurt, pain, and fear resurfaced much later in my life, when I was feeling blocked in my business. Like all this work, business started flowing again after shining a light on these deeper blocks. I also realized it's why I now make sure I have friends in a variety of different groups, not wanting to put all my eggs in one basket. It's also partially my nature with being an only child and seeking out friendships from a variety of different sources. My decisions in business, however, were coming from a fear-based place of being judged and kicked out of the group. This was the culprit behind not wanting to put myself out there in a big way and one that still pops up to this day. Again, the power of the subconscious mind.

Using psychologist Abraham Maslow's hierarchy of needs, love and belonging are right there in the middle of our most important needs. Having a sense of belonging in a group has been proven to not only motivate us but to also help us feel accepted, connected, and safe. This sense of belonging has also been found in a recent study to increase overall happiness and therefore decrease anxiety. And so this need to belong and fit in not only feels good but it also improves our mental health. It's not just about the fear of being alone. It's farther reaching than that.

At a higher, more spiritual level, this is also prevalent. If we believe we are all a part of something bigger, then it makes sense that we have an inherent desire to connect with one another. We crave the connection. This connection with others is how we give and receive love, which is ultimately what we're looking for. It's the *ego* that wants us to stay separate and apart, distanced and isolated from others, constantly judging and comparing ourselves with others. More on that later, but essentially when we say no, we are threatening this driving desire for connection.

We tend to go about it in a dysfunctional way though. We choose pleasing others over our own happiness. This in turn creates feelings of helplessness and a lack of control over our own lives. We become powerless in our own decision-making, breeding resentment instead of the love and the connections we actually long for.

A client came to me once because she was not where she wanted to be in her network marketing business. She was successful in her corporate career but couldn't get the side business that she had been running for a few years to really take off. We started working on the concepts in this book. She realized she had been saying yes to family gatherings too often and was doing it out of obligation. She lived far away and had several young children, and making the long drive so often was exhausting and draining.

After we'd worked together for a short time, she began to consciously decide which events to go to and which ones to say no to. She started setting boundaries. Soon after she began saying no, she was in the grocery store. She thought that she needed to go down the yogurt aisle. She almost didn't go because she didn't even *like* yogurt but decided to follow this thought anyway. Well, lo and behold, she ended up connecting with an amazing person, who later joined her business! All because she became empowered and changed the state she was operating from and allowed herself to embrace her own intuition and instinct. She had the mental space to see it and accept it.

When we start saying no, we put out a powerful energy to the universe. We are saying we are *worthy* of creating lives we love. And we start getting loving opportunities back in *all* areas of our lives, not just business results.

In terms of business, we also need to understand that our fear of saying no is also directly related to our fear of *receiving* a no in business. Put simply, it feels *horrible* when someone turns us down. We take it personally. We don't want to feel like we've done something to someone and are therefore a bad or unworthy person as a result. Are you picking up on a theme? This is what the *ego* wants us to think. We are going to go over the ego and all its grandiosity in an upcoming chapter, but for now we will begin to shine a light on it. It's the judgement we're afraid of, and we're trying to avoid this awful feeling of *not enoughness* once again. We avoid getting a no and stop ourselves from taking the action we need to take to grow our businesses—*sales*! This is exactly what our subconscious wants us to do—to stop when we feel threatened.

After a few years of being in business for myself, I finally learned that sales was the missing strategy. I was doing everything I could to make my business successful, except making sales calls. So I took a course on the subject, which helped me begin to make great headway with sales calls. I was asking bold questions and seeing results. Somewhere along the way, I realized something was off, though, when I got nos from people. My conscious mind was able to say, "But there are seven billion people on the planet, and I can't possible help everyone, so it's *okay* to get a no every now and then!" I would continue on.

But being turned down started to chip away at me, becoming more and more difficult to *talk* myself out of the disappointment I felt with every rejection I received. I started going down one of those *doubt spirals* again, worrying about when the next no would come. I experienced the anxiety about how I was going to earn the money I needed to keep my business afloat and the lifestyle our family had grown accustomed to. The doubtful thoughts led me to question why I was even in business for myself if no one wanted to work with me. Poor me! Complete victim mentality, ridden with doubt, fear, and anxiety—definitely not what I wanted to manifest. Thankfully, I had the awareness—and that strong-willed determination I've spoken about before—to get help with what was going on in my subconscious mind, and when I did, I discovered something utterly fascinating.

As I mentioned the primary feeling I experienced when I got rejected was *disappointment*. When I traced this feeling back in time through the belief breakthrough exercise we did in chapter 1, I discovered this feeling led back to being disappointed when my dad moved to other countries during my high school and university years. He decided to teach overseas, and with that I realized I felt abandoned. No wonder I was trying to avoid this feeling in a business setting and wanting to give up on sales calls. *Who wants to feel abandoned?*

Let's understand—and even embrace—the fact that this feeling of abandonment was just another spoke in my *not enoughness* wheel, stemming from my deep-down core belief system. My own feelings of abandonment were the result of powerful decisions made in my past about not being good enough or loved enough for someone to stay.

Ugh, is this stuff ever hard to work though? It's why running a business is *truly* the best personal development course you can ever take.

How can we shift all this? Redirect these negative dynamics, mindsets, and old belief systems? Again, it's about affirming (and creating) *new* beliefs and making decisions from this newer, stronger, more productive place as though you already believe them. I'm a good example: I was able to see how my old belief system and how that mindset would creep in when it was time to make sales calls, but with work and intentional effort, I was able to tell myself it was an old story and then reaffirm the new and empowered belief I wanted to have instead. I pushed through, and I made those dreaded sales calls anyway, *even* when I felt like throwing in the towel. Eventually, as a result, I started having meaningful interactions with people. I was no longer afraid. I could just show up from a "How can I help you?" place.

Something else interesting also started to happen once I shifted my approach and began to see positive results: I showed my subconscious mind I was in fact *safe* with making the sales calls. And not only safe but also grateful to be truly helping people, which created feelings of love and connection, which was my true (and original) intention of having my coaching business. I was also able to reframe my outlook on sales by witnessing how impactful these conversations were for people even if they didn't sign up for coaching. I can't tell you how many emails I would receive afterwards from business owners saying those conversations were so eye-opening that they went on to double and triple their businesses. And so I began to cherish connecting with people in this way and actually looked *forward* to it. What a shift!

Saying no to people is a lifelong lesson and takes us to deeper depths the more we do it. This isn't easy work. It's usually a little rough when we first start out, so cut yourself a break as you get started. We sometimes start off a little angry after we've realized just how much people-pleasing we've done. I almost think it has to be this way to give us the fuel to start doing it. Unfortunately, this does show up in our communication with others and can be a little (or a lot) abrupt. Just know this going in and give yourself some grace as you go. We also have to remember it will take time to change our belief systems. It also takes the people in our lives a minute to catch up. They are also used to us showing up and responding in a certain way.

Let's look at creating your version of saying no. What can no sound like when you actually say it out loud? Some examples are "I'm good" (taken from my daughter's playbook), or "That's not going to work for me, but I appreciate you asking," or "I won't be able to make that work." Jot down your version now. Then think about one person you've been avoiding saying no to, and commit to addressing them this coming week. Like always, to make it happen, assign a date and put it on your calendar.

If you're unsure if you want to say yes or no in the moment or can't think of something to say on the spot, you can also say something like, "Let me check my schedule and circle back." I find the more I set boundaries in my life and over my time, the less I want to commit to too many plans up front. I don't know how I'm going to feel in three weeks, and so I'm not going to commit to long-term social plans. My husband and I have been practicing this for years after a time in our lives of booking every single weekend full of plans for months out at a time. It was exhausting, to say the least. Especially for us empaths who are absorbing everyone's energy.

It's also important to realize that usually the person asking something of us is just looking for a simple yes or no answer.

Think about yourself. When you ask someone for something, you most likely just want to know if it's a yay or a nay. It's typically our own selves that attach all types of stories to it and feel obligated to justify and apologize and explain. Practice pausing and counting to ten after you say no, and allow the other person the space to respond. You will start to see it's really not a big deal, and it's just that core wound being triggered for us around saying no to begin with and nothing to do with the other person. Eventually, your subconscious will start to see it's safe, thus reprogramming your subconscious mind through your new emotional reaction. And if someone truly isn't respectful when you say no, you may want to take a deeper look at the relationship. It might be toxic or dysfunctional. If so, you're going to need firmer boundaries with this person in terms of how much time you spend with them and how much you allow them into your space (if you allow them in at all).

There is also a lot of buzz right now around the notion that *no* is itself a full and complete sentence. It's actually not though. I do believe the intention is positive with this catchphrase, with the point being we don't need to explain why we're saying no. But there is definitely a way to soften this up a little without explaining, as I have mentioned above. I've found this is especially significant if the relationship is important to you and also if your answer is a no now but might not be at a later time. I suggest being as respectful, compassionate, and loving as possible and using full sentences.

Let's move on to boundaries! This has also become a hot topic, but what does it even mean? Well, setting a boundary is basically a way to protect your time and energy. It's where we set parameters around what we are allowing into our lives.

Think of it as creating a bubble around yourself, with you in complete control over who (and what) is allowed to come into that bubble. Creating this protective bubble around you is a wonderful affirmation that you actually have a say in determining your circumstances. *This is where we step into our power and make empowered decisions for ourselves.* We talked about clearing out the clutter in chapter 3 to have more time and energy, and as a next step, we need to become more aware of what we are letting in and out of our mind space moving forward. This *space* is ever-changing: We might love to go to a family gathering one day and not be feeling the invitation the very next week. It's all about tuning into what is important to us *in the moment*, then consciously making choices moving forward.

Living in proximity to my parents and also my in-laws gave me ample opportunities to practice setting boundaries. With the help of a therapist, my husband and I realized just wanting to stay in on a Sunday night counted as *having plans. Gasp.* We did not need to explain or justify what we were doing; a simple "that doesn't work for us" was good enough. It was us who needed to have a shift around it being okay to take a stand for what we wanted to do. Did it mean we never went to family gatherings? No. But we *did* start making conscious decisions around the usage of our time and what was important to us, and when we did show up, you can bet we showed up much happier, much more relaxed, and a lot less resentful.

As I continue to explore boundaries, I see how profound and far-reaching they are. As you start to say no more often to what's no longer serving you, you will be ready to explore these boundaries on a deeper level. This is where we look at *everything* that is draining our power. Maybe you're with a friend who always talks about themselves and leaves you feeling like you never quite measure up. Maybe you do everything for your kids, talking yourself into it by thinking this is your way to show them love or because they won't be living with you for much longer, but it all keeps you in a place of anxiety and sometimes resentment. This is another sneaky way the subconscious mind keeps you at arm's length from your empowered mode of operating; it talks you into "stopping" and taking on other things instead. The kid one is a big one because it knows exactly which chord to pull to ignite feelings of guilt and parental inadequacy. From these negative vantage points, we know now that this is not the most empowered way of making decisions. We have the power to make conscious choices about the decisions we make.

Of course compromise is important too. Sometimes we will say yes to doing something for someone else because we want to do it for them, even if it's not something we would have chosen for ourselves. Values around family and love do include compromise. We just need to be aware of how often we are doing this and asking ourselves if it's an empowered or disempowered decision. Just tune in as you go. And no, you don't need to go to every single activity for your kids! Sometimes it's okay to take a couple of hours for yourself instead. This is all about making conscious choices.

Let's tune in. What are *you* saying yes to? Is it people and projects that truly inspire and motivate you? Or are you simply saying yes out of a sense of obligation? We also want to look at how you are conducting yourself within your business. For example, you might be working with a client you love but are allowing yourself to be available 24-7, which creates a depletion of your energy and deepens feelings of resentment. Go ahead and jot down everything that comes to mind that pertains to giving away your power. Identify the people, places, and things that are taking up precious time that you could be spending differently.

I see this come up for entrepreneurs from all walks of life, in all industries, this idea of needing to be available for your clients entirely throughout the day (and the night). Many people talk themselves into it under the mistaken assumption that this is their way to provide great service, but on a far deeper level, it is the fear of losing these clients that is actually driving those decisions. Remember that this is your business, and you get to run it the way you see fit, hopefully in a way that is both helpful for your clients *and* empowering for you. If you bring feelings of resentment or even just low energy, it will be felt. Just like happiness and joy are felt. Remember: what we put out comes back. If you're making decisions based out of fear, more in your life will show up that matches that fearful, anxious vibration.

I always like to say if a client doesn't have good boundaries and you're frustrated, it's actually on *you*. It's always up to us—up to you, that is—to show people how you want to be treated. The other person doesn't know, and it's just an opportunity for us to communicate and grow. The frustration deep down is present because we feel uncomfortable speaking up, and this discomfort makes us less likely to do so.

Years ago I started including in my coaching contracts that I would honour additional support for private clients in between coaching sessions within business hours, from Monday to Friday. That way my availability was addressed up front, and the expectations were set entering into the coaching relationship. It didn't come as a surprise if things got off track, and I had to remind a client.

This also brings up another great point: just because someone reaches out to you outside business hours does not mean you need to respond or even address it. The beauty of being in business for yourself is that you get to set your own customer service parameters and do what works for you. Does it mean you won't ever take a call outside business hours? No. But you will be much more conscious about making decisions around your time. You can also set your office hours, where maybe you do take client calls in the evenings, say once or twice a week. The client does not need to know this is what you're doing. This is for your own internal use and inspired living only. To the client, it would be presented as "I'm available Tuesday evening at seven o'clock," for example. Do what works for you and your business.

This also applies to your personal life. Who decided you have to return text messages immediately? Or even at all? If you read Glennon Doyle's bestselling book *Untamed*, you will remember she doesn't like text messages and doesn't respond to them. Ever. She literally has thousands of unreturned texts! This is about looking at what does and doesn't serve us in our lives. So go ahead and think about your own policies and practices around communication in both your professional and personal life. Again, this may take some training for both clients and friends because it's a new version of you coming to town.

Even though setting boundaries does involve a lot of saying no, it also creates the space to say yes. Yes to the people and projects that light us up. Yes to living a life we love. Yes to operating from a place of courage, confidence, and clarity. *When we make conscious choices for ourselves, we're really practicing self-care and self-love at the highest order.* You are tuning into your own needs and what makes you happy. When you operate from this place, you absolutely will have more to give others. Nothing beats giving from an empowered, loving place; it creates a sense of abundance. Your cup will overflow. It is the best feeling and creates the most loving and harmonious relationships in *all* areas of our lives. Every time I start to feel off-balance, I realize I've slipped back into old patterns and have taken on too much, saying yes more often to everyone else instead of saying yes to myself. This is a constant work in progress and one that will always require attention and dedication. Just like staying fit and healthy requires consistent attention. The journey is continuous.

Another tool to help you consciously tune in to what you are saying yes and no to is to identify your own *core values.* When we know what is important to us, deep, deep down, it makes it a heck of a lot easier to say no to what isn't in alignment with those values and yes to what is. It is liberating to say no to the people, activities, and opportunities that are not in alignment with our values and saying yes to those that are. We put out an energy of empowerment and self-love as a result. You are *worthy* of this love and get back more to be worthy of. Like results and dreams.

I remember a time when my son was little and had been invited to a birthday party. It was a busy time for us; we had plans almost every weekend. With one of my core values being family, it was important to me to have downtime as a family and say no to any more plans. This *birthday party* friend wasn't a superclose friend of his either, so it felt okay to say no. I practiced saying no without justifying, with a simple "Bummer, we can't make it."

And guess what. It worked. It felt so empowering. Taking a stand for what was important to me and for my family. Over the years I've been trying to show my kids it's okay to have downtime and to stand up for their *belief* that it is important to have time to themselves in a way that aligns with and complements their own beliefs. We continue to practice this to this day, with them now being teenagers, and I can tell you they have taken notice. Last year my son was invited to a party and said no because he had just been travelling and wanted some downtime. Be still, my heart. Seeing my kids practice these principles, often doing a better job than me, brings me great joy.

On the resource page, there is a fun values exercise that will help you identify your top three values. You can find it at www.chrisatley.com/resources. Go ahead and do this now, or make time on your calendar to go back and do it a little later. You're also welcome to jot down your top values now if you don't want to do the exercise. Some examples are love, family, freedom, fun, and integrity. (Hint: Those are mine. And yes, I did go with five.) Create your own rules. Our values can also change and evolve over time, and like most of the exercises in this book, this is a great exercise to revisit.

Once you have identified your top values, let's look at creating an empowered calendar that supports them. Where do you need to tweak and shift what you're doing so that your decisions about your time align with your values? It's important to note that this applies to both work *and* home life. For example, if family is one of your values, but you are putting clients first all the time by taking calls at all hours, you may need to set some boundaries with client communication. On the flip side, if financial freedom is a value, but you're not sticking to set work hours, you may need to set some parameters with your partner and family. Block off time on your calendar to recognize and honour your values, and start tuning into them when you are making decisions about how best to use your time.

You now have clarity on what is important to you and have a plan for creating an empowered schedule that incorporates your values. You are giving yourself permission to design a life you love accordingly, where there is room for your own needs and those of your clients and family. This is self-care at its highest order.

COACH APPROACH

If you are trying to figure out what is blocking you in sales (aside from not wanting to come across as *salesy*), I am going to take you through an exercise in which you will move around a bit physically. This exercise is designed to help you figure out the blockages in your own subconscious mind that are preventing you from saying no.

It's actually the same exercise we did in chapter 1 but in a little more detail. You will see that this exercise is helpful anytime we feel blocked in some way. I'm going to take you through it again here, and then moving forward, you can come back to it as often as you like.

1. Go ahead and stand up. It can be anywhere on the ground out in front of you, as long as it's not in the empowered

space you mapped out in chapter 1. We're going to dig a little deeper this time, so make sure you are working with your individual timeline. In chapter 1, we made the assumption that in terms of your timeline, the past was behind you, and the future was in front of you. Check in and see if this resonates, or is your past and future more of a left to right or right to left for you? Or sometimes people picture themselves going from down to up, which in that case you would do this visually instead of physically moving.

2. Think about a time when you received a no in business and it really left a mark, meaning it was upsetting and caused a lot of heavier feelings as a result. Good. What is the main feeling you feel? What is the one word you would use to describe this feeing? Make sure it is the predominant feeling. The root of all other feelings.

3. Close your eyes, and allow this feeling to take you back in time, to your earliest memory of experiencing it. Go with whatever memory pops up. Breathe into this feeling, even if it's uncomfortable. Physically step back in time (or over) to the time of this incident. What was going on? Summarize it in your mind. What important decisions were you making about yourself? About the people involved. About the world in general, if that is important? Ask yourself what the positive intention was in forming those decisions. What were they designed to do? Write down all the decisions you made and also the positive intention.

4. Now that you have figured out what important decisions you made, we are going to move on so that your *adult* self, with all its wisdom, travels back in time to have a pep talk with this younger version of you. Decide now if you would

like to take a step back (or over) in time to just before this incident or even earlier in time. Anything goes here. Once you have decided, go ahead and take a big step back (or over) to as early in time you would like to go.

5. Allow your adult self to go back in time and have a pep talk with this younger version of yourself. Just envision it happening. Have your older self share all the truth and wisdom it has to lend your younger self about this incident. Also have your older self share any knowledge, information, and tools that will help this younger version of yourself thrive throughout life in general. Good job. Write down the main things your adult self shared with your younger self.

6. As this younger version of yourself, fully embrace this knowledge as the truth with a few deep, grounding breaths. Bring this knowledge with you by walking forward (or over) into present day, and notice how you are shifting your perspective around old incidents as you walk through time. Keep walking until you are back to the present.

7. Take a few breaths once you are back on the space on the floor representing the present moment. Fully embody all the wisdom your adult self just shared with your younger self, realizing how it will help you in the present *and* in the future. You probably feel lighter, as if a burden has been lifted from your shoulders. Also notice how the positive intention you identified earlier is honoured with this newly empowered version of yourself. Great job. You can step out of this space anytime.

You can now see what you have been avoiding feeling around sales calls and what memory has been blocking you. We want to use this moving forward. You can use your conscious mind to remind yourself of this old story and that it is no longer true, relevant, or applicable. Remind yourself, in those moments, of the wisdom your adult self shared with your younger self, and move forward with that knowledge in a way that allows you to stand strong in the present moment. New inspired action creates new results.

5

DON'T TAKE THE BAIT

Managing Negative Energy

"**THERE ARE SO MANY OTHER** qualified experts in my field. How am I ever going to find clients? What if I'm just not good enough? My competitors have hundreds of thousands of followers! Maybe I'm not supposed to run a business after all."

Therein lies that self-perpetuating doubt spiral.

We all know what these thoughts feel like. It's painfully familiar when the negative thoughts start spiralling out of control until you finally retreat to wondering if you should throw in the towel altogether. You think, "Maybe the universe is giving me a sign to stop moving in this direction. Maybe I should just call it quits."

No! The universe is *not* giving you this signal. You're hearing it wrong. What you actually hear is the sound of your subconscious mind trying its best to convince you to stop. It will stop at nothing to push every button and pull every trigger to get you to turn back. "Danger!" it screams, but *don't* listen to it.

One of the most important concepts we've learned so far as we've travelled on this journey together is that it's actually not safe to stop. It's unwise, counterproductive, demoralizing, and destabilizing. To stop growing, to stop short of doing what you need to do to reach your dreams, is a tragic mistake. Your dreams bring you happiness, fulfilment, and love. Settling for less does not. Cocreating with the universe is the ultimate space to stand in. Don't let your own negative thought patterns push you out of that space. Sometimes it's tempting to listen to the thoughts of self-doubt—I know from my own experience and from working with clients—but you must learn to lean into the energy and vibrations that will move you forward, not backward. Don't succumb to the temptation of self-doubt. I'll put it simply: *don't take the bait.*

We learned in chapter 2 that it's about shifting your vibration so that you can see things differently and take a new action as a result. But where do these thoughts come from initially? Why does this have to be so hard to begin with at every step along the way? We've talked about the law of cause and effect and that our thoughts are the cause of all the effects we see in our lives. But where do these heavier thoughts *originate?* Where and how are these thoughts born?

I started studying A Course in Miracles in 2008, and it's ultimately what helped me heal that core wound. All the exercises I've taken you through up until this point were definitely integral to my growth process in terms of shining a light and gaining insight around the belief systems that were impacting the decisions I was making as an adult, but they also opened me up to something bigger to be understood. After I began studying the principles introduced to me in the movie *The*

Secret, I knew there was more to the story. I had been studying everything I could get my hands on at the time, with coming across other pivotal teachings on the universal laws, the power of our mind, and even angelic support and communication. Bare with me, I promise we won't get too whoo-whoo!

I'll never forget when we went on a family trip with my mom and stepdad early on in my *spiritual awakening*, as I call it. This was before my daughter was born and just before my son's first birthday. As you will recall, my dad passed away when my son was not even a month old, and so at the time of this trip, my spiritual path was just being ignited. I didn't realize this at the time, but I was asking questions around what happens to us when we die and essentially what the meaning of life is. I took an interest almost immediately in the concepts of us living on past death and that there might be more to what we can see beyond the naked eye.

I started reading a book about angels. I was fascinated. Fascinated that not only could we manifest our heart's desires as I had learned from other books but also the *possibility* of life existing beyond what we could see. I became transfixed but terrified at the same time. What did this mean in terms of my own life? Well, this information ended up flipping my world upside down. While I was on this family trip in the Azores, I felt *highly* uncomfortable. I was trying desperately to figure it out, and it was all—and I mean *all*—I could think about.

I started bringing these concepts up over family dinners, and every time my husband and I snuck off for a coffee on our own, I would broach the subject. Bless him for all the conversations he's endured over the years! These concepts were intriguing, yes, but they also had me ridden with anxiety.

Looking back, I can now see my entire paradigm and belief system was being threatened, and my subconscious mind was flashing the red-hot "Danger!" sign in bold, bright lights.

Everything I believed to be true about the world was coming unravelled. It was scary, and it's yet another example of "getting comfortable being uncomfortable." As you've probably started to experience, when we begin changing our thought patterns and belief systems, it is highly uncomfortable. We have built an entire life and thought system around these beliefs, and when we start to change, grow, and evolve, it's threatening. Even though I borrowed some of these books from my mom, it wasn't really something we discussed until I started reading them too. These principles also weren't accepted by anyone around me at the time, and I remember getting into some pretty steamy debates when we would go out for those dinners. I was trying to make a case for something I knew to be true deep down, but it was so new that I couldn't explain it properly.

Sidebar: Everyone around me is now fully on board with these principles, with my stepdad even *Wayne Dyer-ing* parking spaces when he needs one. (Which means taking the spiritual principles taught by Wayne Dyer and *manifesting* a parking space and visualizing it with such intention that it actually becomes available.) So keep going. Keep growing. Keep discussing and exploring your evolving belief systems with others. Your growth sends out a powerful ripple effect towards those who are ready, even if they don't seem to be at first.

I had to put the book down during that trip after it caused so much unease, and I decided to leave it for a while. Along the way, I read several other books about the same principles, but they were a little lighter in their presentation. One by one I shifted my perspective. I circled back to the book that initially caused so much discomfort a few months later and was amazed that the content didn't even phase me. I thought, "This makes total sense! What was the problem before?" Ha!

This work is like peeling back the layers of an onion. With each layer that's peeled away, there comes a *letting go* and a shift in perspective. With each layer that's peeled away, we begin to remember who we really are at our core—a core that has been there all along, awaiting our eventual return.

This is what A Course in Miracles teaches us. The miracle is the shift in *perspective*. A shift in perspective from fear and lack to one of love and peace. Not a romantic love but an unconditional love. Think about the type of love you have for your kids and even your pets. It all comes down to letting go of the thoughts no longer serving us that distract us from having ultimate love, peace, and abundance.

This is the kind of love that connects us all and shows us we are a part of something larger than ourselves. Where we are the utmost powerful cocreator with this universe (insert your own belief system here—that is, God, Source, the universe, Creator, Buddha, and so on), and it's our *true* nature to create joy and love because this is what we represent and are at the highest level. An eternal spirit or essence of love, if you will.

What gets in the way of this? Well, as we've learned, it all comes back to our thoughts. It all comes back to recognizing and becoming aware of those heavier, darker thoughts so that we can let them go. The ones that want to keep us judging ourselves and others. The ones that want to keep us trapped in a state of anxiety, doubt, and *never enoughness*. The ones that want to keep us separate, isolated, alone, and lonely.

Introducing *the ego* in its finest form. My biggest transformation from studying A Course in Miracles has been recognizing the ego and seeing it for what it truly is. It's with this awareness that I was finally able to move past my deep core wound of not being good enough. I finally had clarity on what was truly blocking me. And it goes far beyond belief systems and how we were brought up.

I have spent a lot of time, money, and energy on personal development work over the years. I mean a *lot*. I was always seeking the answers for both business growth and spirituality. I wanted desperately to figure out the law of attraction and apply it to my business and lifestyle dreams. One year, and this was after investing in and attending several high-level mastermind groups and business training courses, I decided to invest $100,000 to work with a mindset coach at the highest level at the time (outside of Tony Robbins).

You may have just thrown up a little in your mouth. I probably did, too, when I decided to do it. But as you've seen, I'm all about going for it. And so I did it. And although I made some massive mindset shifts, especially around money, and I would never take back this experience, the ultimate lessons came when I *stopped* working with this coach.

During the last couple of months of my program, I was struggling to make the payments, even with growing my business exponentially, and so I had to finish early. The way it was handled was harsh and abrupt, and it left me feeling alone. In the weeks to follow, I discovered I was codependent—codependent in terms of always looking for the answers *outside* myself. Of course, we want to keep learning to improve ourselves, but this was different. I wasn't thinking for myself. I was putting all my power with other people. I was looking for reassurance from everyone, including my husband, mom, coach, and friends, and never truly trusting *myself.*

I dove into A Course in Miracles in the weeks to come with my best friend, and together, we explored the course's truths. What we learned was both life-changing and life-defining, namely, that we are all the same regardless of our economical, racial, and cultural differences or social status. This new knowledge was *everything* for me. What it helped reinforce was the notion—no, the *fact*—that more successful people were not any better, smarter, or more deserving than me. In fact, I would soon learn that they, too, suffered from the same *not enoughness* deep, deep down inside themselves, which showed up for them in their own unique ways. Once I started working with many (hundreds of) entrepreneurs—thousands if we count speaking and trainings—I truly saw this was plaguing every single person. It was fascinating. I also saw that I, too, was not any better than anyone else, including the homeless person down the street. It was both humbling and empowering and also inspired working with the homeless youth community in San Diego.

When you truly see this for yourself, it will set you free. You will no longer have to prove yourself in any way, shape, or form. You will also start to connect with others on a much deeper level because you will have ditched the need to be superior, which goes back to low self-worth and inadequate self-esteem. The ego has a spectrum, with one end being where people do not stand up for themselves and the other end being where people are boisterous, arrogant, self-serving, and self-righteous. All grounded in a lack of love.

Once I finally saw this truth, I was able to strengthen this knowledge within myself, and my mode of manifesting—let's call it "creating"—was forever changed. Where it evolved to the point of just thinking, "I would love to work with a new client," and someone would just show up. *This* is how I've created opportunities such as giving a TEDx talk, speaking on the same stages as some of the mentors in *The Secret*; starting a lucrative real estate investing business; and even writing this book. We will get more into the creation process later, but just know this now: There is truly a more *magical* way of living life, where dreams can just flow naturally. Where we can be so in tune with the divine guidance that we do not need to rely on other people. This way of living life belongs to *all* of us. All we have to do is access it. How do we do this?

First, we need to become vitally aware of the ego and how it operates. Per A Course in Miracles, the ego is a thought system. A thought system that is rooted in *fear and lack*. It's that part of us that has us comparing ourselves with others, with never measuring up. We're always lacking something, whether it's more training or followers or letting our kids have too much screen time. We *always* fall short in the eyes of the ego. It's that part of us that feels guilty and inadequate, the part that tries to convince us that we're bad. It's that part of us that wants to shrink and be small. It's that part of us that feels isolated and separate from the group. It's that part of us that is ridden with doubt, worry, and fear.

When we're operating from our ego, we also get self-righteous in our beliefs to protect them. We protect the rules and the rigidity we have formed around our tightly wound operating systems. Where we are right and everyone else is wrong. We resist and defend our positions on how the world works with the same intensity as if our kids were in danger. Why? Because we're trying to escape those feelings of fear and inadequacy. Where we shrink and hide and never want to be exposed for fear of being found out as the bad person our ego would have us believe we are. Where we fight to stay right so that we don't have to be a bad person. Where we shame and blame. Where it rears its ugly head over and over again. Where it's *never* enough, no matter what we do, how hard we work, or how much we accomplish. We reach a goal, and it's still not good enough. We spend time with our kids, and we're still not good enough parents. We eat well and workout, and we're still not skinny enough. Where we're never smart enough to play in the arena with people who are more successful than us. Where we stay afraid and continually second-guess ourselves. Where we analyse and cannot make a decision. Where we question this way or that way until the cows come home. Where we never fully trust ourselves. Where we stay separate from others. Where we keep running on that proverbial hamster wheel with unloving and fear-based thoughts circling around us. Where we believe we're in a body for good and that we die. Where a good number of our decisions can be traced back to this one primal fear: death.

Yikes! This is scary! And how does it show up in our lives? It shows up *in every single area*. Because it's a thought system. It's the inside projecting out. And so we see a world of suffering. Whether it's suffering on a more significant level like poverty or suffering because someone cut you off on the highway. It's all suffering.

On the flip side, through the course, and many other spiritual teachings, we learn this is absolutely *not* who we are. While the ego will have us believe we are contained only in a human body and our lives are finite, this ancient wisdom presents another perspective, one where we expand *beyond* a body. Where we are also (in addition to being a body) a soul or a spirit, an essence that is love and eternal at the highest level. One that is already perfect in its nature and therefore not lacking anything.

And while this book isn't about reteaching A Course in Miracles, or other spiritual teachings, it is important to share this higher truth so that we can have an understanding of what is really going on to let go of the thoughts no longer serving us. It's where the phrase "be of the world but not in it" comes into play. When we apply this truth in our everyday lives, it allows us to have a broader perspective of the world and not take the bait into all the suffering caused by our thoughts.

It's this bait, as I like to call it, that the ego dangles in front of us to pull us into operating from that *not enoughness* place within our thought system, the place that just takes us down a deep, dark doubt spiral as we've seen. We can *learn* to be more careful with our ego. By becoming more aware of how it manifests in our daily lives, we can actually disarm it.

Here's a *quick list* of ways the ego shows up in business:

* Comparing yourself with others in your industry
* Undercharging for your services—or not charging at all
* Having poorly defined boundaries
* Being afraid of losing clients
* Being afraid of not finding clients
* Being afraid to say yes to new opportunities
* Avoiding making sales calls

* Overscheduling your time
* Never having enough time
* Not taking time for yourself
* Not allowing yourself to spend quality time with your kids
* Grinding and hustling
* Staying in overwhelm
* Thinking you have to do everything yourself

Think about your decision-making from this place. When we put out an energy of lack and fear, we manifest that same energy in our lives. If we can recognize this is happening *in the moment*—as we're doing it—we give ourselves the space we need to shift it, and when this shift occurs, we let go of the suffering. We let go of the anxiety and fear. We become clearer and more confident. We can see it for what it is and let it go.

I love the poem "The Guest House," by Rumi. This poem has helped me tremendously over the years. It talks about human emotion being like a guest house, with the different energies, especially the heavier emotions we feel, showing up like guests. I like to think of it as the ego showing up in one of its many disguises. Usually disguised as people in my life who were triggering me in some way. I would picture extending an olive branch by welcoming every single person into my home, who had been bothering me in some way, and then all of us sitting around the dinner table enjoying a meal together. At the end of dinner, I visualize myself saying goodbye and good night to them, then walking them out. This helped me offer acceptance and compassion to them and myself for getting triggered. I saw us all as connected, and it helped me let go on a deep level. This visual always helped me see it was actually me operating from the ego and projecting it out to the people in my life, and there was always something for me to heal inside myself. When we get triggered, the irritations are just a reflection of how we're feeling on the inside and something to heal within. They show up as this or that person doing something to us, but really it's about the lens we're seeing others through.

Think about any situation in your life where you have felt hurt or unheard. Imagine approaching the situation with the awareness of the ego about what's really happening. That this *not enoughness* has been triggered. This is where we take the ultimate responsibility for how we are perceiving the world. If we are reacting, it means we have been triggered and are in our ego. *If we can see it for what it is, then we can let go*, and when we let go, we give ourselves space for the miracle to occur. If we can respond and not react, offer love instead of lack, *imagine* the outcome instead.

I'm definitely not saying we get rid of the ego entirely—that's what true and full enlightenment would be—but we can get faster and faster at catching it and shifting it. I always like to say this is the best measure of the personal development work we've done—how quickly we can shift our ego and redirect our thinking and, as a result, redirect our behaviour. Situations that would have taken me weeks, even months, to let go of now take a couple of days or hours. Sometimes I am able to *release* a situation immediately, as it is unfolding, which feels indescribably good. Remember this: In every single second, *we have a choice*. To choose either fear-based thoughts or loving thoughts. We can take the bait, or we can let it go. We can react or respond. It's a constant work in progress.

How does this play out in our day-to-day lives? I'll never forget a situation I faced at home quite some time ago. We'd just made an insurance claim for a flood we had in our home. Even with me handling these kinds of claims in my past life, the situation still, unfortunately, became adversarial, in terms of restorative work not being covered that I felt should have been. We moved through it, and when all was said and done, we were presented with a big invoice. For something that really was on the insurance company to cover.

After resorting to my old ways of raising my voice to get what I wanted to no avail, I laid off. I settled myself down. I said a prayer to the universe and asked for help: "Please show me the best solution for everyone involved. Please show me what action to take." The guidance was to let it go. It was a feeling—an intuitive hit, if you will. To have trust and faith in the universe. And so I did, and I felt so much peace knowing that I didn't have to carry this burden around. Lo and behold, I *never* heard about it again! It disappeared! Literally not once was it mentioned ever again. We never received another invoice or a peep about it. And that was years ago. Am I saying that problems just disappear all the time? No. But energetically, it was this shift to peace that created more peace back. The most abundant solutions are presented to us if we will allow them in.

Here is a chart to illustrate the ego versus our higher true selves. You will see that it all starts with our thoughts and that there is always another thought to choose, particularly when we are tempted to reach for more negative thoughts.

Ego	Higher Self
What if I can't afford my bills next month?	I am a powerful creator, and the universe is showing me more abundance.
I am afraid this client won't renew.	The universe is showing me who needs my help. We are being brought together like magnets.
I'm not spending enough time with my kids.	I choose quality time with my kids over quantity and have the best time with them.
This friend/colleague/family member was so rude!	They were doing the best they could with the tools they had. I forgive them. I forgive myself.

Now after having reviewed this list carefully, identify the top three disempowered thoughts you've been having lately. Go ahead and write them down. Now think of the opposite; think of an empowered thought for each one that you can think to yourself—and tell yourself—instead. Let's add these new empowered thoughts to your daily mantras. Repeat these thoughts to yourself. Changing your focus and consistent repetition works with the ego. The shift here involves consciously deciding which thoughts to have and choosing thoughts of love and empowerment versus fear. Remember: what we put out comes back.

I once worked with a client who realized her ego sounded like the character Janice from *Friends*. Remember her loud, high-pitched voice? The voice that was bossy and demanding? (Sorry, Janice!) All kidding aside, this voice *is* relentless in its quest for evidence of *not enoughness* by showing us *shoulds* and *have-tos*. It's a louder voice than the wisdom of our higher selves. When I'm talking about *voices* here, don't worry, it's not schizophrenia. Or at least it doesn't mean it is. The loud, ego version is the judgemental voice, the thoughts that are harsh and constantly critical. Our higher selves, that inner wisdom or intuition, is softer and quieter. It's more of a knowing. Either way, when I say voices, I'm basically referring to giving your *thoughts* a voice. If you pay attention now, you will discover what I mean and realize our thoughts really *are* like voices.

With work and practice, we can start to catch which thought systems we're listening to. Are they loud or quiet? Judgemental or accepting? Eventually, you will start to see the difference and can make decisions accordingly.

But back to my client. This particular client became so aware and in tune that she could spot the ego for what it was and see exactly how it was trying to throw her off in business and life. Often disguised as the *next best* business idea, really it was the ego trying to keep her in a constant state of anxiety and overwhelming stress with trying to implement all these *great* ideas. She was able to start making conscious choices from her higher self by tuning into her intuition instead, which involved self-care at an even deeper level.

She began to incorporate painting and nature walks into her work schedule because she knew these activities led to an empowered state of mind for her that in turn would be the caveat to creating more flow and presence in her life and business. I should note this was after breaking six figures in her coaching business in record time while practicing lots of self-care. Meaning she was able to identify and then achieve a whole new level of self-discovery after making time for herself and treating herself as a priority on an even more substantial level.

When we learn how to not *take the bait* and move ourselves through heavier emotions, we truly can live a more fulfilling and freeing life. Where our thoughts no longer have such a tight hold over us. Where we can hear the quiet guidance of our intuition that is part of a bigger system at play, one that is always supporting us. Where we can enjoy connecting with people on a much deeper level.

Does all of this mean we won't still get upset? No. It's not about *never* feeling heavier emotions; that is not our goal. We don't need to try to be perfect all the time. (We are going to delve more into that in the next chapter.) Putting a spiritual Band-Aid over our old wounds is not helpful. We need to allow ourselves to feel how we feel and then look at what triggered those feelings. This helps us feel the feelings, then let go of them. Sometimes it's those feelings of great pain that lead to the most healing. That is love. Judging ourselves for how we feel is the ego. Moving forward, let's up our awareness and continue to shine a light on the ego and its limited thought system that is coming from fear and lack—anything but love.

COACH APPROACH

The following exercise is great to use when you want to see yourself, someone else, or a situation differently. It helps us *let go* on a deeper level. Essentially letting go of the pain and discomfort that often take hold of us and prevent us from having more love and peace in our lives. It's these types of situations and the accompanying judgemental outlook that hold us back from creating what we really want to be creating.

1. Take a moment and remember an argument or a situation in which you were intimidated or a situation in which someone did something that resulted in hurt feelings on your part or even a situation in which you held you back in some way. Choose a situation that is mild to moderately unpleasant.

2. See the situation play out in front of you. Identify yourself in the situation and the other person in the situation and where they are standing. Create spaces on the ground that represent both of you. Where you are standing now, looking at both of these spaces, will be considered the neutral, observer space. Watch the situation play out in front of you from this neutral, observer's perspective.

3. Now step into the situation in front of you by stepping into your own self (space) on the floor. Replay the situation again and see things from your perspective, taking note of all that you are hearing, seeing, and feeling from your *own* point of view.

4. Now step into the neutral, observer position. Watch yourself and the other person with detached curiosity and in detail. Notice how the other person sounds, looks, breathes, and behaves. Consider any information you have about their values, personal history, and experience immediately before the event you're remembering.

5. Now step into the other person's (space) on the floor. *Become them* as fully as possible, adopting their physiology, perspective, history, and mindset, replaying the situation in your mind fully and completely from their point of view.

6. Step into the neutral, observer position. Watch the interaction between the two people again (you and the other person) with the information from both of the other positions available to you. While reviewing the entire situation again, bring all the knowledge and perspective you have gained by looking at the situation through different lenses.

7. Ask yourself the following questions: What has changed for you in relation to this memory? Which position was the easiest for you to take? How might this shift be valuable in your work moving forward? In your life?

Enjoy this shift in perspective and lightness you feel. Noting the work you did was all about shifting how you see yourself, the other person, and the situation. Nothing else changed! It's incredible. How will this mind freedom create the space for you to cocreate with the universe? What can you put your efforts towards now instead?

Go for it!

6

BE THE NUCLEUS,
NOT NUCLEAR

The Perils of Perfection

YOU'RE RUSHING, RUSHING THROUGH THE day so you can finally get some time to yourself. You've worked a long, full day; picked up the kids; made it through the *witching* hour (4:00–5:00 p.m.), when kids seem to turn into tiny monsters; made dinner; cleaned up; and finished bath time, and now you're wondering when you can sneak out of the room after tucking in your kids to *finally* have a moment to yourself. But either you fall asleep in their room or you're asleep the minute you start reading a book in your own bed. You wake up in the morning reprimanding yourself for failing to meet your personal development goals, and then you repeat the daily cycle all over again. Ugh.

At least this was me, anyway—always setting myself up to feel bad, and never quite measuring up to the rules and expectations I had for yours truly.

We've talked about the ego, but the way it shows up as perfectionism deserves its own chapter so that we can address it fully.

Why was I so hard on myself? I remember a coach I once hired saying to me that I needed to cut myself a break. That I was way too hard on myself. Easier said than done, though, right? To just *stop*. Boy, if only it was that easy. That was my first eye-opener into this toxic need for perfection. I started peeling back the layers of the onion by doing the deeper belief work and by also bringing in the awareness of how the subconscious mind operates.

Where did this deep-seated need for perfection come from? Always trying to do so much, achieve so much, and *be* so much. Never resting, always hustling. What the heck? By this point, I was well versed in work-life balance and with even having achieved a self-care routine, but it quickly became just one more to-do item on the never-ending to-do list, as I mentioned before. I filled every crack and space of time with *something*. Tasks that just *had* to be done, I'd convinced myself. And not only did I fill those free spaces of time; I also doubled up on them! Racing, doing, rushing, moving from one task to the other, squeezing in every idea and task that I could think of in record time. I looked at other women who did not operate this way with complete judgement. I'll be honest. I judged their ambition and drive (or what I thought was lacking of both), and I wore mine like a badge of honour. My inner voice was screaming, "Don't *they* want to be successful? Why can't they just get it *done*?"

Wow. Not a train of thought I'm proud of. But one that is all too common within us recovering perfectionists.

So what gives? Where does this need for perfection come from? Why are we constantly trying so hard to be flawless? We get caught up in chasing the dreams that will ensure our external success (and the lifestyle that comes along with it). We hustle, hustle, and hustle at being the perfect mom, the perfect wife, and the perfect human being. We are relentlessly trying to *be* a *good* girl, to get that gold star.

We ladies were brought up to be good girls. Am I right? Be kind. Be nice. Be polite. Be subservient. Put everyone else's needs (and opinions) before your own. While I was growing up, my mom was always telling me to be polite and respectful like Lady Diana (yes, Diana, the Princess of Wales). No tall order, right? I'll never forget the time when I was a teenager visiting my aunt, my mom's sister, and we were driving down a back-country road in Canada. We pulled over to a hole-in-the-wall gas station, and I cracked the joke, "Would Lady Diana stop here?" Ha! I mean, if you're going to use her as an example, let's go all the way!

My mom's intentions were good, as are most parents, but that constant quest for perfection leaves a mark. I understand now, knowing what I know, that this need for perfection was a belief system passed down from society throughout the families in our generation.

What drives this need for perfection we've all bought into?

Well, what I discovered about perfectionism—and you're probably a recovering perfectionist like me if you're reading this, or at least striving to be—is that perfection is grounded in wanting love and approval from someone outside ourselves. Where we are constantly doing and achieving to try to get that love and approval. Whoever just popped into your mind as you were reading this *is* that person for you. Don't judge it; just go with it.

The reality is that you have given so much power over to this person. They have become your singular source of reassurance and praise because that is how you have learned to get love. Reassurance being a way to get love from others. But the funny (and not-so-funny) thing about this is that the love and approval you're seeking from that one person never seems to come anyway. I'm not saying that this person doesn't love you—I'm sure they do, in their own way—but it's that their reassurance never quite measures up to your expectations. More often than not, you probably end up feeling *more* anxious than you did before you sought out their reassurance. You reach out to them looking for this love and don't quite get it back the way you want it, anxiety-producing (and demoralizing) in and of itself.

And that is the powerful deception of reassurance—always falling short and never quite measuring up.

Why is that?

Because you're searching for love in the wrong place. Remember in chapter 1, where we talked about how society conditions us to look for our worth outside ourselves? Well, that's what's happening here. Of course, we still want to check in with other people, bounce ideas off them, and learn from them too, but it's the intention that's behind it that matters. If you're trying to obtain your own sense of self-worth from them, the response you get from them will always fall short, no matter what their response is. It's another ego trap, and it's disguised in seeking love. Except we're always looking outside ourselves for this love. Never tuning inward, always searching outward.

Remember: what we put out, we *always* get back. If the energy we put out is rooted in lack and fear, we get back more energy that strengthens those feelings of lack and fear. In this case, it's lack of love. It's important to note here that it's not that it's what we're actually receiving back; it's what we're *seeing* as a result.

Remember the universal laws we went over in chapter 2. We are in that lower vibration and therefore see the world this way. Even though there are opportunities to see (and receive) love all around us.

This is where our knowledge about the ego is important. The ego is always wanting us to feel like a bad person at the end of the day, as less than and not good enough. It tells us all kinds of stories about how we did or didn't do this or that well enough, that we're not a good enough mom, friend, wife, and so on. And so we keep striving, striving for that love and approval, because at the end of the day, that is *all* we want, to be loved. And so we will take on a gazillion projects at work and around the house while proudly being the room mom and the perfect wife at the same time. We will do *all* these things and pretend we feel great about it. And we actually are proud, but deep down that resentment is simmering, slowly coming to a boil.

So what can we do instead? Well, we're working on creating a new and empowered belief system, right? We are affirming our new beliefs every day and also have a deeper understanding of the ego and its thought system. And while that is all well and good, what can we actually start doing differently?

Flip the script.

When I realized I was rushing through the day to finally get some time to myself (which never fully worked out because by the end of the day, as I've already mentioned, I was too tired and would fall asleep), I took definitive action: *I changed the time of day for my self-care.* Thank-you to my own coach at the time! One of those *duh* moments, but it's hard to see our own blind spots sometimes, which really is the whole purpose of this book—to shine a light on what keeps us in a disempowered place, whether it be the most seemingly smallest thoughts and actions.

I changed my self-care time to the mornings *instead* of the evenings. I started getting up before the kids (and my husband) and had the whole place to myself. This was everything. Not only because I could now fit in my self-care time but also because it drastically impacted how I felt all day. I realized I was starting my day being filled up, focused, and *tended to*, and this felt amazing. I was happier, which translated to my having more patience with the kids. I also wasn't rushing through the day to get to this time for myself, with that resentment brewing at bedtime because it was all I wanted to do. I could enjoy story time. I took the pressure off my own rules of getting it all done. I started measuring up—not measuring up to others but measuring up to *myself*.

Looking back, I realize that this was a complete act of self-love. Loving myself enough to put my own needs first. Realizing that when I did this, it was not selfish. It was *necessary*. Realizing that when I took loving care of myself, I moved from nuclear to loving nucleus. So much more love and grace to give to my family.

And gradually, this undoing of perfectionism and rules and expectations started to become unravelled. Gradually, I began to extricate myself from the web of lies I had bought into. I began to set my *own* terms of how households (mine) should be run, along with navigating spouses and relationships, parenting, and business. I began to take control of my role as a daughter, wife, friend, mom, and member of the larger community. I began to control and determine for *myself*, ultimately, how I gave and received love.

When we first moved from Canada to California, I put a lot of pressure on myself. I continued on with a few coaching clients and was also trying to get our life set up here, which was no small feat, given that I had to help establish our identities in this new country and create an entirely new physical environment. This was while having two small kids (they had just turned four and one) a month after we moved. But I couldn't complain, right? This was my dream come true.

At first, I naively believed there would be no stress to go along with creating this massive dream. I believed I could handle this move flawlessly, whatever that meant. As I started doing more and more belief work, I realized the story I was telling myself was that my husband expected me to have everything running *perfectly*. But when I finally asked him, he said, "I just expect the kids to be safe and fed." Oh! It was me (the ego version) making up this *have to be perfect* narrative. It was my ego that was keeping me in never-enough mode. That's how it hooks us.

So what can we do to shift it?

We want to keep shining a light on it. The way to shift your subconscious thinking, the way to redirect that tricky ego of yours, is by asking yourself what stories you're telling yourself and where these stories are coming from. Realizing it's not actually the pressure from society, nor is it the external pressure or expectations from any particular person; it's the pressure from *within*. Sure, we've absorbed information from society and other people and decided it was true, but that was because we decided it was true. Therefore, we can decide to no longer accept it to be true. We get to decide what we believe, and it's this free will to choose differently that will set us free. We do have free will, which is also how we can decide to listen to (or not listen to) the ego, whose lies and deception often keep us in an intricate web of fear and lack. It is from this clear-sighted place where we can really, truly, authentically make decisions; interact with others; and live our lives.

I notice this popping up at every new level I take on in my business. My core wound of *not enoughness* pops up, and I start worrying about what certain people think. Who I'm worrying about depends on where I'm at in my life and who is in it at the time. As we've learned, it's just a projection of the ego, so the *who* doesn't really matter. But my ego sure knows how to convince me otherwise. It will show me the thoughts to hook me into caring what said person thinks. What's interesting is that this downward spiral becomes even worse if I'm not feeling grounded. If I'm a little extra stressed or overwhelmed, which usually happens if I let my own needs start to slide, I'm more apt to listen to the ego. When I allow myself to slip into this place, I notice I am far more susceptible to other people's opinions. And the ego knows just the right angle to show me; the ego knows the precise moment to pounce. All of a sudden, opportunities to say no and set boundaries start popping up all over the place. And it's uncomfortable when I feel shaky. But then I realize, "Ahhh, of course, this makes sense. I slipped into the ego, and I'm feeling off."

Energetically, what's happening is that I've slipped into a place of fearing what others think—this is the energy I'm putting out—so this is the energy I'm getting back. So what comes to me are more thoughts and stories that put me in a fear-based mode of operating, which leads back to being afraid of people's love being taken away. This is why I always say if you're feeling off in any way, *do not go on social media*. It's a breeding ground for *not enoughness* when you feel off (and a great source of connection when you feel on). Where the same post can literally invoke a different reaction depending on the lens you are seeing it through.

You get to decide, and in every single second, that choice belongs to you. This also means you always have the opportunity to reset and make a different choice. You don't have to become fully enlightened or sign up for one more course; you can choose love right now. In this very moment.

How do I navigate the ego when I take new leaps in business? I see it for what it is and make myself take the inspired action anyway. We will get more into this in a later chapter, but I say yes to the opportunity, I push towards it anyway, and lo and behold, I prove my subconscious wrong and see that I am still safe! What's even funnier, something always presents itself to appease the fear I have been worrying about. Either said person shares they also aren't feeling great, or they give me a compliment on the exact scenario I was afraid to put out into the world, or something else happens and I receive that validation from the universe that this was in fact a story.

What does it mean to choose love?

It means to fill up your cup first. Every day, in every situation. It does not mean you don't ever comprise or that you never put someone else first. But when you are making conscious decisions for yourself throughout the day and not just adding in a self-care routine, you become happier and more empowered. You become more and more aligned with love. You have so much more to give others that it no longer feels like a compromise or a burden. It no longer feels like something is being taken from you.

You realize *you're* the one you've been waiting for.

You've been waiting for this empowered, loving version of yourself. The highest version of you that is unconditional love.

That is pure joy and bliss. That is confident and kind, grounded and creative. The most magical, mystical version of you.

You're probably thinking, "Yeah, right. Like that's possible." I feel you. Again, if we felt this way all the time, we would be fully enlightened, which we aren't. Not when we think we're stuck in a body, and this is it for us. Not when we listen to the ego as we navigate this *being human* business. But if we can just get a glimpse of this state, enough to see that it is possible, and start strengthening it while we shine a light on the ego, we can align with it more and more often. It's really not even aligning; it's more like *remembering*. Remembering this is who we really are. Because this is who we have been all along.

And who are we? We are a consciousness that is a part of something bigger, that is connected. Therefore, we are all connected at a higher level. We are accepted as we are. Love. It's so abstract that it is really hard to describe with words because it is a feeling. For me it's when I'm cocreating with the universe. Making the impossible possible and truly living and making decisions as if there are no limits. Because there really aren't any limits at that level. We truly are limitless as a spirit/soul.

One winter I went on a retreat in Peru, which, funny enough, I had a hand in creating. We were finishing up an event in Arizona for a belief breakthrough training I was a part of, and our mentor invited us to continue on with another more in-depth training that would include retreats. Knowing he grew up in Peru, I asked if we could have one of the retreats there. I thought it would be fun to study these principles *abroad*. He loved the idea, so he included it. It was divinely led for sure!

He arranged for the most magical experience, an experience that included working with a shaman and also seeing some of

Peru's world-famous landmarks, such as the Sacred Valley and Machu Picchu. We finished off with the training part of our program in Lima. It was truly one of the most beautiful and transformative experiences I've ever been a part of. I'll never forget the sound of the oversized hummingbirds' wings flapping. The shaman would lead us on the most beautiful hikes in the Andes, where we even had a flautist accompanying us on one of the treks. We stopped for many moments of meditation in those beautiful mountains, but I remember one was especially profound for me.

We were encouraged to wander off for this one and find a special place to sit and meditate. I chose the side of a cliff. All I could feel during the meditation was the word "limitless" and the vastness of the word moving through my body. In that moment, I knew we were truly limitless. It helped that all I could see when I opened my eyes were rolling, majestic mountains in the most vibrant shade of green that never seemed to end. It was a spectacular moment and a feeling I'll never forget. It's this feeling that I'm trying to describe to you here with words.

How do we strengthen this limitless self-love state that we want to remember? I remember actually googling how to find self-love! How funny. I was like, "Where is it, and how do I get it? Is there a course, a teacher of such things?" And while I do think courses and information can help, it really comes down to it being an inside job. What lights you up? What makes your heart sing? Just do that. It's as simple as that and yet as hard as that at the same time.

Does it mean you have to make drastic changes right now? No. I find the whole "find your life purpose" thing interesting. I was trying to find my purpose for years when I first got into personal development and actually before that with saying to myself during my insurance days, "I just want to feel passionate again." Here's the thing with that though: It's not something you *find*. It's something you tune in to. It's about allowing yourself to do what makes you happy in all areas of life. Does it mean quitting your job or going down a new path professionally? Maybe. But maybe not. It's amazing what happens when we start doing more of what we love in our personal lives. We become happier, and this shifts how we see everybody and everything, including a less-than-stellar work environment. I say start there, and then see what conscious, empowered decisions you make from that place.

Start tuning into your own needs every single day. Make it a habit. Maybe things need to shift in your household or in the way you operate your business. Is it empowering? I also love the question, "What would love do?" a question a good friend of mine turned into a spiritual card deck. If we ask this in any given situation, it's never going to be about lack. Either for you or for someone else. The most loving solution might be to set a boundary with someone so that they, too, can see it's okay to set boundaries in their own lives. A win-win. I think about this all the time with my teenagers, which incidentally feels a lot like the infant stage. With cutting up fruit and veggies again so they will actually eat them and saying no when they ask for more money. What have you done to earn that? It's a never-ending process and a form of constant self-evaluation, this act of deciding what we feel is loving and appropriate at the same time. But with a little awareness, we can go a long way.

Self-love is truly about tuning into our own needs and desires. It's about strengthening those decisions and operating from that place. Maybe you want to light a candle during your work time or have a bubble bath before you flip to mom mode at the end of the day. Maybe you want to take on new and empowered business projects? Maybe you want to fill yourself up with a great podcast while you make dinner? Every single decision we make counts. Do we still have the mundane tasks that go along with being human? Of course. But how can you make more empowered decisions around them? How can you make your life more fun and *funny*? Let's remember how powerful humour is in changing our state and remembering not to take ourselves so seriously. I'm talking to myself here too. Do you need to take a break your own rules from time to time and let go of the rigidity around them? Do you need to lower (or, at the very least, adjust) your expectations of yourself and others? These acts of self-care ultimately strengthen our love for ourselves. Where we say yes to valuing ourselves and no to underestimating ourselves. Where we say yes to *enough* and no to *not enough*. Where we allow self-love to extinguish the perils of perfection. Where we finally arrive, armed with self-respect and a self-cherishing like no other.

I realized my expectations were just an ego play to keep people at arm's length. If they never measure up, I don't need to be vulnerable and love on a deeper level and risk being hurt; it keeps "Critical Chrissy" always fired up and never quite satisfied. It keeps her safe. Or so she thinks. How often does this beauty pop up around expectations with family members and even with our own kids? Think about something that bugged you and is likely that she or he did or didn't do this or that. Where we're always determining who is right and who is wrong, but it's just not our job to be the general manager of the universe. I did not see the job posting for this. It's time to let that go and see the ego for what it is. Always wanting to keep us separate. Never wanting us to truly love or remember who we are at our core. Always trying to trick us into the belief that we must be perfect.

Let's do a little check-in. What is a grudge you are holding on to right now? What is the story you are telling yourself about this grudge? What is the expectation you have that is causing the thoughts about who is right or wrong as it concerns this grudge? How do you know this expectation is the truth? In the previous chapter, I took you through the perceptions exercise, which can also be helpful for grudge-worthy situations.

Another great visual that can also help is to close your eyes—after reading this, of course! Picture the situation and then allow yourself to elevate far above it in the sky, where you can see yourself and the other person involved. Zoom out as high as you need to in order to let go of the charge you might be feeling. Great! Look down at the situation, and ask yourself, "What is the lesson to be learned here?" There is always an opportunity to grow and learn when we get triggered. We just need to take—or create—the time to examine those opportunities.

It's amazing what happens when we operate from a more neutral and loving place. We become more grounded and confident, and this is felt by everyone around us. We get caught up in less drama, and the need for reassurance diminishes. We trust our own selves and the decisions we make. We judge people less in this place and observe things more. We let challenges, roadblocks, and hindrances roll off our backs to a greater extent. All those little nigglies we feel start to fade away.

And this can be *felt*. Imagine how the quality of your relationships will improve when all this starts to shift. You will feel lighter, and you will have room for more meaningful relationships. You will feel more connected. It also becomes a lot easier to say no and set boundaries. You will become stronger in your resolve. It's addictive to take a stand for yourself and create a life of peace and happiness that you love. You never want it to end. And the good news is that it never *does* have to end. You are in complete control of this goodness.

COACH APPROACH

The following exercise is one of my absolute favourites. It's a great exercise to do anytime we are facing an internal conflict. Where we might feel pulled in two directions. For example, the pull between wanting to be a good mom and run a successful business is constant until we can reconcile that inner turmoil. Let's use this exercise to help in the healing of this now:

1. Think about the conflict between working and parenting. If that isn't a conflict for you, then choose something else. You can do this exercise sitting down. Identify at least two opposing sides (parts) that are causing an inner conflict; there is usually a positive side and a negative side or the part that wants to change and the part that keeps enabling the problem.

2. Place your palms facing upward on your lap and decide which palm represents which part, or side, of the conflict. Create an image that represents each part, and visualize these images in the corresponding palms. These images

can be whatever you like; they can be objects, shapes, or colours. Anything goes. The decision, again, is yours.

3. (a) Focus your attention on one of the parts of your conflict first. Ask that part in your hand what its positive intention is for doing what it's doing and why it's showing up. Keep repeating that question on whatever answer you get until you arrive at a positive value such as love, freedom, joy, and so on.

(b) Focus your attention on the other part of the conflict next. Then ask that part in your hand what its positive intention is for doing what it's doing and why it's showing up. Keep repeating that question on whatever answer you get until you arrive at a positive value such as love, freedom, joy, and so on. Even if one side feels heavier than the other. There is always a positive intention deep down.

(c) Notice that what both parts want (their highest positive intention) is either identical or compatible. You must get to this point where they are the same or compatible before moving on. Continue to ask questions about this until you do.

4. Now start with one part, and ask it what resources and tools it can lend the other side to achieve its highest positive intention. You may need to remind yourself what the other side is trying to achieve, then ask again what resources this side has that it can lend to the other side. Then do the same with the other side.

5. Now turn your palms inward to face each other. In a second, picture each side now *sharing* all these resources with each other. Do this for both at the same time. Both sides sharing

the resources. Go ahead and begin, and at the same time you're doing this, turn your hands so they are facing each other and move your hands towards each other as if you are actually sharing the resources with both sides. As your hands come together, create a third image that symbolizes the integration of the two parts coming together and aligning as one.

6. Bring the newly integrated image over the top of your heart by placing both of your hands on your chest, breathing it in and absorbing this whole new experience in your body, mind, and spirit while picturing the third image surrounding your chest. Good job.

7. Relax for a few minutes and then think about that old issue in light of being a more fully integrated person now. Think about how you will approach this situation in the future.

You probably gained some insight as to how the two sides can actually work together to achieve your ultimate positive intention. After freeing yourself of the burden of having to choose one side over the other, the inner peace you are looking for comes with this alignment. Moving forward, you can use this exercise anytime you feel that inner conflict arising or when you're stuck in indecision.

Remember, again, that you can *choose to choose* which direction, which belief, and which patterns of self-care you want for yourself. When you do this, and when you truly turn inward to seek that ultimate self-love, you'll discover that your need to constantly strive towards perfection will evaporate.

And when this happens, you are no longer nuclear.
You are the *nucleus*.

7

BE INTENTIONAL

*Meaningful Ways to Set Your Goals
and Actualize Your Dreams*

BY NOW YOU SHOULD BE feeling light, aware, empowered, connected, confident, unstoppable. Way to *be*. You have taken your power back and have created an empowered way of *existing*. A place where you are truly seeing your value and embracing your worth. Where you have identified the belief systems and ego thought patterns no longer serving you. Where you are *aware*.

This new sense of awareness, as powerful and motivating as it is, brings us face-to-face with something that Canadian journalist Amanda Lindhout describes with perfect clarity: "With awareness comes responsibility and choice."

This newfound responsibility could be seen as a burden or as the ultimate *freedom*. When we become aware of the truth and who we really are, we realize we truly do have a choice. A choice in what we are creating, what we choose to see, and what we choose to participate in.

Most of us have been taught to let our circumstances dictate our decisions instead of making the decision to do what we want *first*. For example, when I was growing up, anyone moving geographically to follow their dreams was pretty much unheard of. These types of moves were saved for those relocating specifically for work. That seemed to be the only acceptable reason for wanting to move away from family and friends. From familiarity. We see yet again another example of other people's long-held, outdated belief systems dictating our reality.

When we start pulling back the curtain on our limiting belief systems, we realize none of this is true. We absolutely can create our heart's desires, and we absolutely can follow our dreams, even if the pursuit of those dreams moves us to another location and even if our pursuit ends up disappointing others. One of my mentors used to say, "Do you want to manage a life of regret or move through the fear of following your dreams?" It's a legitimate question, as it is ultimately up to *us* to decide. We still have free will.

Hopefully, you are at a place in your journey now where it's a yes for you to bring your dreams to fruition. It is our soul's purpose to create. We have the right, the privilege, and the capacity now to create abundant *soul*-utions for ourselves and to set into motion the title of this very book. We have the ability now to create love and joy and expand that love and joy outward to others. When we live this way, doing what we love, we also give *others* the permission to do the same, including the very people we were worrying about disappointing to begin with. I can't tell you how many magical memories we have created with family over the years in California that we wouldn't have had if we had stayed put. This act of cocreating is freeing and inspiring for everyone involved.

The first step is to give yourself permission to go after your dreams, no matter where those dreams take you. Permission and decision are one and the same. Permission to do what makes your heart sing is a *decision* in itself. You are saying yes! When you allow yourself the space and the freedom to decide to go for it, you then get a powerful ball rolling not just within your own mind but throughout the *universe* because you are clear about what you're asking for. The universe loves clarity and will start aligning to give you what you're wanting. Remember: the universe speaks in feelings and vibrations, so it's the energy of what you're asking for that gets put out there and therefore what will return to you. If you're wishy-washy in what you ask for because you're living in indecision, you will get back wishy-washy results, causing you to further doubt and therefore strengthen this indecision mode of operating. You are in control, not the circumstances presenting themselves. As we already learned in the preceding chapters, *like attracts like*.

Along those lines we also want to be aware of ego-based goals versus higher-self dreams. This can get confusing and even contradictory in the personal development world. Messages such as "Money doesn't make you happy," but then on the flip side, "You can create massive amounts of wealth!" Hmmm, conflicting messages to say the least.

What I've learned from travelling my own spiritual path and business-building journey is that money is *okay*. Money never did anything to anyone. Money itself is inert; it's the judgements we place on those who *have* it that so often create conflict and imbalance. As we've learned we are deathly afraid of being a *bad person* deep down, or being seen as a bad person by others, and therefore want to avoid being judged at all costs. And so we flip-flop back and forth on whether it is or isn't okay to want money, sending out mixed messages to the universe all along the way. It's not a coincidence we get muddled results back from the universe as a result. We cannot stand in fear and faith at the same time. Remember: it's the *feeling* that dictates what comes back to us.

I'll never forget the time we decided to lease a BMW. I was so embarrassed pulling up to my son's preschool in it. I started explaining and justifying why we got it to anyone who saw me. Fast-forward to living by the beach, where not only BMWs and Land Rovers are the norm but where Bentley and Ferrari sightings are also quite common. And I can tell you no one is apologizing to anyone. You can see how our ego could go to the other extreme—explaining why you don't have a good enough car. Geesh! The ego is forever criticizing and never satisfied, which creates constant inner conflict. In business, for instance, we clearly say we want x, y, and z, but deep, deep down, we do not want to be judged for having wealth, a.k.a. being a bad person.

But it's not the money that makes you good or bad. It's all about your intention and where you're coming from to begin with and the decisions you make about how to use your money when you do have it. Remember the exercise we did where your money could communicate with you about how it's being treated? Would it have good or bad things to say to you? Hmmm . . . for a lot of people, it's even a reflection of what it's like to be in a romantic relationship with themselves. It's truly fascinating.

How do we decipher between ego-driven goals and soul-creating dreams then? It's all about tuning in and asking ourselves what our intentions and our motivations are. Do you want to redo your kitchen because you feel yours isn't good enough? Maybe you're trying to keep up with the Joneses next door? Or is it because you want to create a beautiful space for your friends and family to gather and a comfortable, inviting place to share meals and deepen heartfelt connections? You can see how those two intentions are very different. Do you want that new purse because you feel like you have to keep up with the styles and trends, and therefore how you're receiving your worth, or is it because it's something you love and expands that beauty and joy outward? Very different intentions, right?

Let me back up a second. With that last example, it's not the *purse* that brings you happiness. It's more that you already feel happy, and you are allowing yourself to extend that out to your external environment. To whatever brings you more joy and happiness. Allowing yourself to be surrounded by beauty in whatever way that looks for you. For some, that may be a new purse, for others, a home that has a breathtaking view of nature. There is no judgement. You do you, knowing it's okay to desire material things, as we do live in this world filled with forms. It's more about asking yourself why you want it to begin with and realizing *things* and forms don't really bring us happiness. Happiness is an inside job, and we're just extending it outward. That's really the difference between ego-driven goals and soul-creating dreams. The ego is always searching for external affirmation and accolades; the soul already knows it's enough and wants to share.

It's a slippery slope between not enough and good enough when we're setting goals though. Remember from our explorations in preceding chapters that the ego *voice* is always loud and boisterous, telling us this or that isn't good enough and that we need to strive for *more, more, more*. This is the voice that tells you we're always lacking something and need more to satisfy it. Whereas the *higher self* speaks in whispers. The higher self does not need to shout. This is the voice—these are the thoughts and ideas—that tugs at our hearts. It is never demanding; instead, it is filled with an intuitive knowing. A knowing that the idea being shown to us is about enhancing joy and expanding it outward. It's repetitive and comforting; it is always waiting for us patiently. Ideas and thoughts we know we need to honour and pursue but don't always take the action. For our higher self, it's never about *getting*. It's the *receiving* of these ideas and thoughts that allows us to create. Creating makes us happy, and when we are happy, we expand that love and happiness outward. It's that ripple effect again.

The best way to set meaningful goals is to tune in to your ideal lifestyle. What do you love to do? Who do you want to do it with? What does your ideal business and schedule look like? When we get real with ourselves, we realize our financial goals have less to do with getting accolades for reaching a certain level in our businesses and much more to do with the *why* behind those financial results. This is about setting meaningful financial goals that are in alignment with how we want to live.

Let's do an exercise. Give yourself about thirty minutes to do this. Choose an inspired spot, and grab your favourite journal. Write your ideal lifestyle out like it's one year from now and you're looking back over the course of the year. Include the date as you begin. Write it like you are thankful for everything you've created and grateful for all that has transpired over the course of the last year. I recommend handwriting this versus typing it on your computer. Writing by hand provides a direct link to your subconscious, therefore deeply rooting what you want inside you. Plus it forces us to really slow down and feel what it is we are wanting to create.

Get as specific as you can in all areas of your life. The more specific you get, the more you really start to feel like you've already achieved it. This is important for visualizing (more on that in step four). Let's allow those daydreams to flow.

The following questions will help you get even clearer on your ideal lifestyle. If it's helpful to step back into the empowered place on the floor that we identified in chapter 2, please do so. Either way, let's invoke that empowered state of mind by standing in it or thinking about it—remember the word you chose—before tuning into the following questions. Remember to write your answers as if they have already occurred:

* What is important to you? What do you want to be, do, and have this year?
* Do you want to do something fulfilling?
* Do you want to give back?
* What do you love to do?
* What brings you joy?
* Where do you want to live (i.e., geographic location, the type of home, etc.)?
* What characteristics does your ideal environment have? Is community important?
* What type of support is important at home and in your business?
* Do you want to travel? How often and to where? Do you want to bring anyone with you?

* What types of activities do you want to participate in? Is providing them for your loved ones important?
* Are you responsible for all, most, half, or another percentage of your life with someone else (i.e., mortgage, utilities, housekeeping services, etc.)?
* What else do you want to make time for in your life?
* What type of self-care practice is important?
* What is your health like? Do you have lots of energy?
* What do your relationships look like?
* What does your time with your kids look like?
* Are you involved in your community?
* Your savings—what does this area of your life look like, or what are you on your way to achieving?
* Are you financially free?
* What does a freedom-filled life look like to you?

Once you've finished writing this out as if you're looking back over the past year, go through what you identified, and assign a monetary value to everything you mapped out. Remember to include your current expenses and what it will cost to run the business you ideally would like (i.e., proper support, setting aside money for taxes, etc.). Go ahead and add those to your ideal lifestyle if you didn't already include them. Add everything up to arrive at your desired annual income, then break this number down into quarterly and even monthly numbers. This is your new, meaningful, financial goal! Woo hoo! Probably a bit of an eye-opener, right? You can now work towards putting a plan in place to make it happen. We want to start doing what we can now in this very moment while allowing the rest to unfold.

It's also important to identify what feelings you are trying to create by manifesting your external goals. Now that you're clear on what you want to create, ask yourself what feelings that will give you once you've achieved it. Now think about how you can invoke those feelings *now*. Remember: we are a *feeling universe*, and it's not about waiting to feel that sense of freedom, peace, joy, and so on until your external goals are achieved; it's about allowing yourself to feel them *now*. And amazingly, once we do this, we actually attract to us what we're wanting even faster. Remember: it's all about creating from the inside out. What we put out comes back. Always.

The second step, and this is a biggie, is to proceed with following your dreams without knowing *how* you're going to make them happen. It's this step that I see a lot of business owners getting tripped up over. With not even *allowing* themselves to dream big because they are too busy staying stuck in the worrying of *how* it's going to happen. Most people know what they want deep down, but it's the uncertainty of how it will come to fruition that stops them in their tracks before they even try. We want to shift to a place where we make the decision *first* based on what we want and allow the how to show up *second*. It's completely opposite of what most of us have been taught, but the universe is ready to show us the way. We just have to *trust* that it will be shown.

Letting go of the *how* was my biggest breakthrough in creating inspired goals, and it continues to be. Following dreams that seem so big and insurmountable, where we're forced to get out of our own way and allow something bigger to take over. To guide us. To lead us. To support us in bringing these dreams to fruition. It is the ultimate letting go of the ego. The ego just doesn't have our best interests at heart, but the bigger whole does.

For me, this seems to be around real estate investing. My first experience with this involved buying our home in San Diego. Even though I had bought and sold multiple homes in the past, this one presented itself from seemingly impossible circumstances. Initially, we were told no multiple times by several mortgage brokers. But because of the principles discussed in this book, I knew there *had* to be a way. Per the universal laws, for every *problem*, there has to be a *solution*. I was firmly rooted in the principle "If there's a will, there is absolutely a way."

And so I pushed through. Beyond the ego. Well, I just *happened* to meet a mortgage broker at a business networking event. He saw a way to do it, he saw a way to get around the problems we were having, and this opened up just enough of a crack in the window for me to see there was going to be a way after all.

The universe (driven by my own determined will) led me to another mortgage broker in our area, and I proceeded to have endless brainstorming sessions with him and the people on his team. There was no way I was giving up, even though he, too, told me no multiple times. Well, lo and behold, the ways to *make it happen* started showing up. One by one. From new clients to a raise for my husband, to credit scores dramatically increasing in rapid time (this had been difficult with being from a different country), to even getting insights from neighbours who were in the business. All these new windows began to open up one by one.

I would literally think, "I need to go for a walk," and just *happen* to run into someone who would give me the next bit of information I needed to move forward. It was incredible! Every single detail aligned for us to make the purchase possible. It was so outstanding that our mortgage broker joked at the end of the home-buying process by saying he was going to frame our approval letter because he thought there was no way it was going to happen. We also ended up having the most spiritual conversations along the way, talking about how anything was possible, and by the end of the process, he was even quoting the ancient Chinese philosopher Lao-tzu. This mortgage broker has since become a friend and is always willing to entertain and brainstorm my crazy ideas, with even stepping in to save the day on my latest endeavour while writing this book.

This is what lights me up. The *creation* process behind the dream being actualized, although the dream coming to fruition is great too. It's the *ideas* that push me so far beyond my own pre-conceived limits that truly have me surrendering. Surrendering to something bigger. To trust that this all-encompassing universe and the guiding source is leading me and is always showing me the way to make these creative ideas happen, thus reinforcing and strengthening my belief that anything and everything *is* possible. That we truly are limitless. Because we have access to something beyond us. Beyond what we can see. After so many examples of this in my own life and in those of my clients, I just cannot look the other way. Where clients and colleagues have created massive business results in record time. Where clients have manifested lifelong dreams of living in different countries. Where business owners have generated speaking events and book deals. Where entrepreneurs have produced investment properties and TEDx talks! All the while practicing plentiful amounts of self-care. Think working smarter and not harder. *Tune in.* What do you need to tell yourself about your dreams?

What is the empowered belief you need to embrace to conceive them? Per the subconscious work we've learned, repeat it often.

The third step is to keep saying yes, even though it's scary as hell. I always ask, when I'm speaking to groups or individuals, "What came first—the chicken or the egg?" Meaning, do we believe the empowered belief that we identified first, and then that leads to us creating what we want? Or do we see results first, thus strengthening what we're trying to believe?

I've found it's *both*. We affirm the belief *and* make decisions as if we already believe it. What would you do if you already believed your new and empowered belief? How would you present yourself to the world? How would you dress? Talk? Take action? When we're operating from this place, we then start to create different results, thus strengthening the belief. And so the next time we go to take this inspired form of action—inspired because it's leading us to our dreams—it's much easier to believe it's possible and that the way will make itself known. We are essentially strengthening our trust and faith in something bigger that's guiding us, surrendering to it, and allowing it to show us the way. Surrendering means that we allow ourselves to be led, trusting those ideas and signals, and saying yes to what shows up!

Saying yes to every single step we're shown can be scary until we create more experiences where we see our goals and dreams being actualized. Our trust and our confidence are strengthened with every step we take, and with every step we take towards realizing our goals, we know that we can never turn back, the awareness being ingrained in us forever. This is where phrases such as "take a leap of faith" come into the equation. The steps and ideas will be shown to us, and they will be uncomfortable at the same time because there is an element of letting go.

Letting go of the fear of being judged as we take these leaps. And here's another saying you've heard before: "Let go and let God." Take this one to heart. The *letting go*, as we already know, is letting go of the ego-based ways of operating that no longer serve us yet have become deeply comfortable (and entrenched) within us. The disruption of these old belief systems is highly unnerving. For example, you might be guided to take action and reach out about a speaking event or to set a hard boundary with someone and take a stand for yourself. All uncomfortable but all necessary in actualizing your dreams.

The fourth step is to visualize or to get into the same vibrational energy that aligns with what you're wanting. What I didn't understand for a long time is the notion that this isn't a "one and done" process, meaning we don't just visualize what we want in the morning and then expect what we want to come to us by that same afternoon. This is about a consistent practice around caring for, directing, and managing your energy over a sustained period. A consistent practice of tuning in and looking at where you're feeling imbalanced and deciding how to get back on track. We can't just visualize, although it's certainly helpful, and then expect what we've visualized to simply appear before us. It requires more work than that. *We must actively participate in taking control of our energy.* What we create is dependent on it.

Let's break it down. Why is visualizing helpful to begin with? Well, our subconscious mind doesn't know the difference between imagination and reality. So the more we can clearly affirm what we're wanting and how it would *feel* to create it, the more we can actively create a shift inside ourselves that reprograms our subconscious mind. We are providing consistent repetition with affirming what we're wanting, and we're also creating that emotional reaction we talked about. We don't have to only create *real* experiences in our lives; we can create them in our mind as if they've already happened. This mental work strengthens the empowered state of mind we are wanting to operate from. The more we invoke the feelings associated with already having achieved our dreams, the more we're also strengthening the belief that we need to have to make them happen. When we envision already having achieved them in our mind, we know without a doubt they're possible because we see ourselves as already achieving them. From this place of confidence and, yes, grace, we can make decisions that drive us towards everything we desire.

This is why vision boards can be helpful. This is the process of creating images and words on a board—digital or physical—that represent what we're wanting to create. When I first did this years ago, we tore out pages from magazines and posted them on a bulletin board! Wow, how technology has changed since then! Vision boards help us consistently reaffirm and visualize what we're wanting and to invoke the actual state of what it *feels like* to have already achieved it. It's why surrounding yourself with your mantras is so powerful. It keeps you in the *feeling* of what you desire.

Having a gratitude practice is also a great way to change our state. When we're happy and grateful, we attract more of that to us. It's important to find the gratitude in our lives now, even if we're wanting to change something. Maybe you want to move but feeling grateful for where you are, and what you have *now* will actually lead to that move happening faster. As you can see, it's really about invoking this state of mind and doing it in whichever way resonates for you.

From an energetic perspective, when we spend time thinking about what it would be like to achieve our goals and dreams, it puts us in the vibration of what we're wanting, which is likely love, peace, joy, and abundance deep down, and then we will attract more of that to ourselves or, as discussed, see the next steps there before us that will allow us to bring these desires to fruition.

We need to do more, however. There are other steps to take. We can't just visualize and then slip right back into fear, or listening to the ego, throughout the rest of the day. This is where the real work lies. How do we show up during our day? How do we treat others? How are we making decisions? This ego-busting is a consistent work in progress. As we've learned, at every second of every day, we can choose to listen to—or *not* listen to—thoughts from love or lack. We need to consciously shine a light on the ego, see it for what it is, and choose a more loving way of being instead. This is why self-care and self-love are so important. It's about consistently changing our state. The universe will always give us back more of what we're putting out; we just need to meet it halfway. Consciously asking for a shift in perspective, to see things differently, is super helpful in letting go of those ego-based thoughts.

We also need to revisit trust again, which is our final step. We need to trust that we are being shown the very best way at the very best time. And if something doesn't work out exactly *how* we planned it or wanted it, we need to know it may not actually be in alignment with the larger plan. For example, with real estate investing, I always ask the universe for guidance on whether the opportunities that present themselves are good investments both short term and long term and, if so, to be shown the steps to make them happen because, truth be told, I don't always know what opportunities are good. But the universe does. I do get a *gut instinct* about them, and that's usually when I know to move forward, and from there, I'm allowing it to unfold and trusting it's for our highest good if it continues to. I have learned to put full trust in the universe itself. We will get more into this higher-level process in another chapter.

The opportunity to give a TEDx talk happened in this same manner. I had applied a few years prior with even becoming a finalist but didn't think too much about it again when it didn't come to be. Well, I was doing a meditation a few years later and afterward thought, "I would love to give a TEDx talk!" I ended up hopping on Instagram and saw that a university was hosting one on being the change we wanted to see in the world. It sounded perfect. So I applied. And after an inspired phone call, I actually *got* it. *And* it was in India—literally all the way around the world (if you count coming back). I could feel my ego trying to talk me out of it, saying things such as "But it's so far," and "You're not getting paid." And then I remembered what else I had been asking for: to speak around the world about meaningful topics and to travel with my family. It ended up being just my son and me, who was twelve at the time, and we had the most magical time travelling around India. We saw the Taj Mahal, went to Jaipur to spend time with the monkeys and elephants, and even ended up at a yoga retreat centre in the Himalayas, where my son and I did meditation and yoga classes together! Be still my heart. We also made friends for life.

It's this belief in something bigger that needs to be solidified to release ourselves of the burden of trying to control everything for ourselves (where *hustling* comes into play) and surrendering on a deeper level to allow the flow of the universe to enter. And what I have found is even if people don't necessarily believe deep down that this type of flow will happen for them, they will gain strength in the stories of others. I've witnessed this universal guidance too many times to not truly believe we can be anything we want to be, do anything we want to do, and have everything we want to have. All this is completely possible. It might just look different from what we think, a.k.a. trying to control the *how* of it all.

And something magical—but also very real—happens when we trust in something bigger than us. We shift from trying to get (lack, fear, ego) to truly being of service (love, happiness, connection). When we know we're always being taken care of by a force larger than ourselves, we can truly focus on helping others and being of service to our clients and communities. Where during a *sales* call, we can focus on what the other person truly needs, which may or may not be our services.

And what happens when a goal doesn't work out? It's usually one of two reasons. The first being it wasn't really in our best interest and was more of an ego-based goal to begin with. This usually pertains to something we talked ourselves into or was driven by scarcity, lack, or low self-worth. As we practice tuning into our higher selves and looking at our intentions and motives behind why we want what we do, this ego-based thinking won't dominate our emotions and our resulting behaviour as often. You will get to know the difference between these two types of goals the more you tune in. It's almost like exercising a muscle: the more you repeat it, the stronger it becomes.

The other reason for falling short of a goal is that sometimes we simply slip out of alignment. Sure, we may change our minds as we gather more information or course correct as we gain more clarity, but if it's truly something we want, inspired by joy, and it doesn't come into being, it's just that we've shifted into some type of fear around it. It could be fear of getting it or even a deep-down fear of *not* getting it. Either way, it's based on fear. And fear, as we already know, creates energetic vibrations that are not in alignment with our dreams.

It all comes back to trust. The more we can strengthen our trust, the more we can fully accept that something bigger than us is always guiding us and the faster we become at letting go of the fear and stepping instead into faith. When we're in alignment with the voice that whispers to our souls, we will always be shown the way. In this space, we are cocreators with the universe.

COACH APPROACH

This exercise is great for when you feel fear, doubt, worry, or anxiety about doing something new. You can do this sitting or lying down.

1. Think of a circumstance or situation that creates fear, doubt, worry, or anxiety. It can be about putting yourself out there in a business setting or something else. As always, anything goes.
2. Tune in to that feeling. Where do you feel it in your body?
3. What is the shape and size of it?

4. Is there a colour associated with it? If so, is it solid or transparent?

5. What is its positive intention for showing up? For example, why is it there? What is it designed to do?

6. Then thank it for showing up. Picture a different colour entering your body that is lighter in feeling and there to support you. Imagine this energy moving throughout your body.

7. Notice how the positive intention of the heavier feeling is honoured with this lighter energy and connection. For example, if it was showing up to keep you safe, how are you actually safe?

8. Allow the initial feeling to move through you and dissipate as the new energy fills you up and expands beyond you.

This is a great exercise to remind us that there really is a positive intention within us that is yearning to be heard and seen. Once we see it for what it is, we can let it go. We are feeling the feelings here instead of trying to talk ourselves out of it. This in and of itself is a loving and compassionate act. We can then shift that heavier energy to feelings of peace and love as a result.

All of this is within our reach, within our control, and within our everyday reality.

8

FORGIVENESS

How Compassion and Love Shift the Life Dynamic

THERE'S ONE AREA THAT SEEMS to trip us all up. It's holding on to grievances. A grievance is basically anything that causes us suffering. It can range from being upset about something someone said to being a victim of extreme injustice. It is all-encompassing. It is *all* suffering. And when we hang on to it, it negatively impacts *us*, not the other person or people involved.

Remember chapter 3, where we looked at what you were tolerating in your life. Holding on to grievances is probably the biggest toleration, with it being the ultimate time and energy suck. Think about how many times a day you are judging yourself *and* judging what others do as right or wrong. We've explored in detail the many layers of the ego as we have moved through the chapters of this book, so we already know this with certainty: Once your ego has made a case for self-righteousness, you are given the green light to suffer. Suffering is formed by the judgemental thoughts the ego feeds us, which then lead to feelings of anxiety, doubt, and fear—and it's these feelings, as we've already learned, that make up the ego's playground. This applies not only to simple, daily interactions we have with people but also to the bigger acts of injustice that others (or ourselves) have committed. Whether large or small, major or minor, we must make decisions about how to handle them and how we interact with others. Those smaller decisions we make daily tend to keep us disconnected and in a lower vibration of blame, shame, and criticism simply because they are ego based. They are designed by the ego to keep us isolated and uncertain about who we really are. We internalize and therefore operate with burning simmers of anxiety, doubt, and fear. This is both draining and agonizing, to say the least.

When we're impacted by grievances, it causes a lot of heavy energy, such as resentment, anger, and sadness, to build up, and this energy manifests in our daily lives. We ruminate. We seek reassurance. We replay the sequence of events over and over in our minds. We go back and forth between feelings of righteousness and worthlessness. This, yet again, is the working of the ego. All designed to distract us from feeling good and being happy. To stop us from operating from that empowered place we've been talking about. The ego wants us to stay in that prison of hell. Where we second-guess. Where we doubt. Where we stay stuck in the past or where we worry about the future. Where we *suffer*. Because if we're suffering, we can't be empowered. And if we're not empowered, we will not create the loving life that we are meant to live. And when we've bought into the lies and deceptions our ego is feeding us, we are putting out this fear-based, lacking energy on a deeper level, even if we are not aware of it. Which in turn impacts every area of our lives. They are all intertwined, as we've learned.

So what is the answer? How do we move past this? *Forgiveness.*

What does it mean to truly, fully forgive someone? It definitely does not mean we just go around *loving and lighting* everyone, although that, too, can be a useful energy shift. With deeper hurts, this is hard though. It's hard to just talk ourselves into letting something go. The phrase "talk is cheap" comes to mind. True forgiveness requires us to first *acknowledge* the pain and hurt, and most people shy away from this because it's too painful. But if we skip this important step of acknowledging our own pain, that pain will continue to build up, it will continue to accumulate and create imbalance, and this will negatively impact us in some way, shape, or form in our daily lives. When we try to just skip over it or brush past it, when we create this *spiritual bypass*, we are missing the shift and often the accompanying lessons and are not doing ourselves any favours in the long run. We have to be willing to do the deeper work, the difficult work, to truly be released from our grievances. It also does not mean we condone the act when we do finally let go. It means that we let go of the tight grip the grievance has around *us*. I love Nelson Mandela's quote on forgiveness: "Resentment is like drinking poison and then hoping it will kill your enemies."

A client of mine who was very successful in her career came to me a few years ago because she felt stuck in her side business. She had seen some great success, but no matter how hard she tried, she couldn't reach the next level. We did some deeper mindset exercises and discovered she was hanging on to past hurts with her ex-husband. Once it was identified and she shifted her perspective, she was able to let go of the heavy thoughts and angry energy that was consuming her, see it for what it was, and start moving on. She also wrote a letter to her ex-husband, which I'm not sure she ever gave him, but the very act of writing the letter, putting words on paper and claiming those words as her own, helped her release the ill feelings she had towards him and the events that had unfolded in their relationship.

She felt *free* and unburdened, and it was beautiful to watch. Businesswise, results began to flow again with new clients, and revenue increased quickly, with her even earning a coveted level in her network marketing organization. And it wasn't that she condoned the hurtful things that happened between her and her former spouse, but she was able to *let go* of the hold they had around her heart that was causing her to operate from a place of anger and resentment. The heavy energy of anger and resentment was showing up in *all* areas of her life, not only in her business. It was also present in her interactions with her kids, particularly when those interactions pertained to their father, and it was dictating how she was making decisions and handling logistics. The interesting part? Before we did these mindset exercises, she didn't even think this was bothering her. She thought she had moved on. This is why the subconscious work is so important. It always tells us the truth. Watching this shift in such a short period was spectacular to witness.

This is what forgiveness is. It does not mean excusing the act that has been committed. It's about being able to let go of the thoughts and burdensome energy around our *hearts* to set *ourselves* free.

I was working with another client, who was in the online marketing world, to help her grow her business, and some interesting things came up about forgiveness for her as well.

This client had been abused as a child, and she was holding on to some pretty heavy energy around safety and security and rightly so. How can one ever *let go* of such traumatic events or even think about forgiving the perpetrator? Well, she did, and it was a massive moment for her. I took her through an exercise that actually moved her towards forgiveness; this is the same exercise I will take you through at the end of this chapter. The exercise was useful—pivotal even—because it enabled her to see that her current sense of safety and security was no longer connected to that past experience. It was those past decisions about safety—decisions rooted in her own past trauma—that were running the show in her present-day reality and essentially preventing her from moving forward in her business and allowing true abundance to flow in in all areas of her life.

Again, the subconscious wants us to stop when we feel threatened in any way, and putting ourselves out there in business feels like a very real threat. Not only did she shift (and expand) her perspective on where her safety and security really came from but she also forgave the people involved. Again, she was not *condoning* what happened, but her expanded perspective allowed her to see the people involved for what they were and to fully accept that she was no longer going to tolerate them having a hold over her own life, so she was able to let it go. As a result of her letting it go, her business reached new heights, generating six figures in just three months' time. All because she showed up differently. She was a beautifully inspired version of herself. I was honoured to be a part of this transformation.

In both cases, these women allowed themselves to go deep and were able to facilitate the shift they needed as a result. And it's this shift that we're going for, this shift in perspective (thoughts) that changes our feelings towards someone or something from our past. Instead of fear, anxiety, and resentment, we become filled with love and compassion. We feel free and light as a result. We have created a new emotional imprint in our subconscious mind and have changed the state from which we make our decisions. It's the same shift we've talked about in past chapters, but forgiveness has its own special place.

If we go higher level for a minute and accept the concept that we are all eternal beings connected to something larger than our individual selves, then we can start to also accept the concept that any acts that others, and ourselves, commit out of fear are just that. They chose fear instead of love, to which we all have a choice at any given moment throughout the day. Whether it's getting irritated with our kids or spouse over some preconceived expectation not being met or it's some other larger act of injustice. Fear is fear, and love is love. There isn't an in between. Either you *is* or you *isn't* at any given moment of the day, and we all flip-flop back and forth between our ego and our higher self.

But our higher self is pure love; our higher self doesn't have the capacity to choose fear or acts of injustice or violence. That is the ego's job. If we can see who we all truly are and accept that we have come from the same place, that we are all connected, then we can forgive the acts and decisions made from our fear-based egos. Again, not condoning the acts themselves but releasing ourselves and others of the lasting burden those acts have created in our daily lives and choosing instead to see *the truth*. Forgiveness helps us remember who we really are. Compassionate beings.

This *bigger picture* viewpoint helps us forgive acts regardless of their size, whether they're bigger or smaller. We can take a step back to truly see how the person involved (even if that person is us!) chose poorly. In some cases, very poorly. But it's not who they are at the end of our time here. They are a soul created out of love, but they (we) simply forgot this. We are all guilty of forgetting this *bigger-picture* awareness from time to time, which causes us to get tripped up over grievances. Like we talked about in the previous chapter, we truly are limitless. Imagine if we all operated from this elevated viewpoint all the time. There would be far less, if any, suffering because we would all be operating from a place of love and kindness. Definitely a world I want to be a part of.

And I know what you're thinking because I thought it too: "Well, that's all well and good, but what about more heinous acts of violence? Like murder? How can we possibly forgive *that*?" Please know that I hear you on this. This is something all too familiar for me, and I spent years trying to get my mind around it as I was studying A Course in Miracles and learning about forgiveness. Does it mean it's okay to commit acts of violence because there's more to us than the life we see here? No. Because violence of any kind is not a loving act. That is still listening to the ego. There is an element of letting go of attachments to worldly things and even the death of our bodies, but that doesn't mean not caring and not being loving. It's actually the opposite. How can we bring this loving knowledge into everything we do? Returning to the essential question we've asked ourselves before, *what would love do?* The answer: love would not take advantage of or commit an act of violence towards another, no matter the scale.

We had a very sad and traumatic experience in our family that required me to apply this knowledge in my own life. One of my cousins was violently killed at just twenty-six years old. This was in a tiny and safe town in Canada, and our family and the community were completely flabbergasted. The pain this caused my family was unfathomable. What I worked on for years, and continue to work on, was trying to see how the person who committed this cruel, monstrous act lost their way. He chose very poorly and obviously had a deep unhappiness within himself to conduct such a loveless act. In my own mind, though, I would picture him as a soul, a single part of a larger whole that makes up who we are as a collective unit, and that this hateful act doesn't represent who he is deep down.

I tried, and I still try today, to take this expanded perspective, which helps me understand that he was created from the same love as the rest of us and that this awful act does not represent his true essence. Did this mean I was excusing what he did? No. Does it mean there shouldn't be consequences? No. Was I putting a spiritual Band-Aid over the pain that he inflicted? No. The loss is still heartbreaking. But looking at it from this larger vantage point did help me loosen the vicelike grip it had around my heart, and it does help me practice forgiveness because it allows me to see the truth of who we really all are at a higher level.

This brings up another important point: Just because we have the knowledge of who we really are—a loving, eternal essence—doesn't mean we need to be best friends with everybody. We still want to surround ourselves with other like-minded people who match or raise our vibration, who are not stuck in their ego. That is also an act of self-love, as we have discussed. Sometimes with this work, the ego can try to lure us in with thoughts on the other end of the spectrum, such as "Well, if I truly loved everyone and saw them for who they are, then I should be able to be accepting and therefore around everyone."

Yes and no. Bringing this knowledge into our day-to-day interactions is huge. But so is allowing yourself to give and receive love, to connect with the true essence of who other people are, and recognizing the fact that sometimes other people aren't willing (or able) to connect with who they really are. I could put this another way: *You do not need to fix everyone.* Just your acceptance of where they are sends out a powerful, loving energy, and you can love them from afar. I've fallen into this trap many times, where I want to see the good in people and have made poor choices, unfortunately, with who I do business with. I was trying so hard to shift from my adversarial insurance days, and it was like I was blinded with rose-coloured glasses instead, wanting to believe so badly that the other people involved were pure in their intentions. But funnily enough, something always told me when something was off, but I chose to move forward anyway. I realize now what that *something* was: my gut. My instinct. It never lies and always tells the truth, and when I don't listen to it, something always comes back to bite me in the butt.

Oh, if I had a dollar for every time I didn't listen to my gut and my instincts! But even this act of learning to listen to your gut, and your heart, is itself an act of self-love and compassion, and I feel deep gratitude for learning this important lesson because it helps strengthen my sense of self-love and, ultimately, helps me decide who I allow myself to associate with.

But back to forgiveness being the tool that will set us free. As I already mentioned, forgiveness does not mean we just look the other way when someone has been wronged or violated us on such a deep level. This ongoing journey towards forgiveness can actually take many productive paths and can lead us towards our life's work because it calls on us, ultimately, to expand love to others.

Such is the case with one of my cousins, a sister of the cousin who was killed, who went on to study victimology and now helps empower victims of crime. Her ability to forgive led her towards her life's calling because she was able to relieve herself of the burden of her own anger, resentment, and fear. No, she didn't excuse the perpetrator—what he did was beyond cruel—but adopting a wider perspective allowed her to look at it from a place of higher vibrational energy, and the higher vibrational energy offered her guidance that was positive and productive.

Sometimes this guidance might not be about taking action or doing something. It might be about sitting in prayer and extending love out to others in a quiet, more passive fashion. This may not look like *taking action* by society's standards, but the unseen healing that's taking place shouldn't be underestimated.

Sometimes the *action* you take might be sharing your perspective on forgiveness and helping others realize it's possible. We just need to tune in again to our *intention* and return to the essential questions: Are we coming from a place of love or a place of hate? What is love telling us to do? Take inspired action or ask for a shift in perspective? It's going to be different for everyone, and when we let go of the judgement of what we should or shouldn't be doing, we can freely move forward. When we listen to the loving guidance there for us and have a shift in perspective to love, that is the true miracle.

This work also requires us to take personal responsibility for our own actions and see our part in situations with others. I'm talking more about the day-to-day actions versus a bigger act of injustice. If we can find just 1 percent of where we might be responsible, or even why the situation is showing up or the lesson to be learned, this enhanced sense of personal accountability takes us out of our victimhood mentality and gives us liberty. Even though the ego wants us to avoid this for fear of being a bad person or for fear of admitting, heaven forbid, that we did something wrong (back to our old friend perfectionism) or somehow contributed to the issue, if we can get around our own ego, the results will be truly freeing. That is the empowering part.

Although we've talked about some pretty big issues this far, how do we actually let go of those day-to-day grievances? I really think this is the true work, as this is what most of us are working through, in some form or fashion, in our own lives, at this very moment. It's the tiny judgements we make day-to-day that keep us stuck in this heavier energy and steer us away from creating our heart's desires. These smaller, incremental acts are sometimes more challenging than the bigger acts of forgiveness, simply because it's these minor daily interactions that we are confronted with the most frequently. How we show up daily is a direct reflection of how we feel on the inside. Imagine walking around with a deep-seated resentment. How does our inability to release our resentments come across in our interactions with others? How we feel deep down determines what is showing up in our lives and our businesses, as we've talked about a lot throughout this book. What we put out comes back. *Always.*

This is why when people laugh off their problems as *champagne problems* it's not actually true. These are still real issues. When they are hurtful, this *is* suffering. No matter what the level of pain and problems, it's important to remember: hurt is hurt, and when we judge ourselves for it, it throws us into deeper suffering.

What I learned in A Course in Miracles is that, quite simply, suffering is suffering. There is no difference in the size of problems; just like on the flip side, there is no difference in the size of miracles. Realizing all these grievances come back to fear. We are afraid of not being loved, and so we judge ourselves so that we can be *good*. A *good girl*, for instance, measures up to other people's expectations and gets that approval she's so desperately looking for, but it is approval from others, not from herself. Conversely, we impose these judgements on others as well. We judge someone as wrong or right, good or bad, and then we hold a grievance against them as a result. But really, this is a reflection of just how deeply we're judging ourselves. It's indicative of the expectations we have of *ourselves*. I am now convinced that those high expectations we talked about before are in fact our *limitations*. They keep us in a place of judging, focusing on what that person did wrong, and because we've deemed them as *wrong*, they are undeserving of our love. But we're judging ourselves the hardest, and we cannot love others until we can learn to love ourselves. It all comes back to self-love. When we do not have love, we withhold, retract, and stay separate and guarded as a result.

So how do we move past this? Well, anytime I drift into judger mode myself, I pull back the curtain and look at what is actually being triggered. It's usually something about not being listened to, feeling unheard, and therefore ultimately feeling disrespected. Not loved enough to be listened to—back to that *not enoughness* that we've explored throughout this book. The problem is that if I let that *not enoughness* dictate how I respond, react, and behave, then the ego's got me. I've taken the bait, and it's a slippery downhill slope from there.

I've noticed my ability to not judge and let go is strengthened the more I take care of myself and practice self-love. There is a direct correlation. If we can take the time to ground ourselves regularly in the self-care practices we have talked about throughout this book, we can strengthen a more confident and loving state. When we strengthen our love for ourselves, it changes the way we see the world and expands how we choose to operate in it. This is where the expansion of love, specifically of self-love, can actually manifest in the lives of other people because we shine a light that illuminates outside ourselves. It changes our reactions to responses. We allow ourselves to have more love and compassion for ourselves *and* others. Energetically, what happens is that we've changed our state to a place of love, and therefore it makes sense that we will gravitate towards thoughts of love instead of thoughts of judgement and fear. Remember: the energy we put out always returns.

I am much more likely to see the truth of a situation and others involved, including myself, when I'm in this place. When my inner judger comes out to play, I realize once again I've likely taken on too much and have slipped into an overwhelmed, stressed-out energy level; from this lower vibrational energy level, I see myself and everyone around me as lacking in some way. Critical Chrissy ready to take her place centre stage.

It's not a coincidence that while I was writing this chapter on forgiveness, I had a complete breakthrough moment on what forgiveness actually is. I always thought of forgiveness as a tool. A way to let go of the ego to experience the love of who we really are. I would affirm every morning in my own morning practice that I forgave others (I would picture anyone rubbing me the wrong way at the time) and then forgive myself. Even though this can create a shift inside us and shouldn't be discounted, it really isn't quite it.

What I realized in real time during the recording of our podcast *One Simple Truth*, where my best friend and I discuss all things related to A Course in Miracles, is that I'd fully embraced what forgiveness is on a deeper level. Forgiveness itself is more than an act. Forgiveness is the *feeling* of compassion. Forgiveness is a feeling that in of itself creates the act of forgiving. When we allow ourselves to feel how we do, maybe we wake up in a bad mood or are going through something tough, and when we give ourselves permission to simply *feel how we feel*, without judgement, it's in this moment we have given ourselves love, grace, and compassion. *That* is true forgiveness. It's the shift in energy from fear to love. It's the process of shifting our feelings. It's not something we think our way through; it's the shift in energy that takes place. This is why the mindset exercises I've done with clients are so helpful. It helps shift the energy around the incident. If we trust our analytical mind entirely, we invite the ego to keep us in a place of "Yeah, but this person did this or that . . ." and this analysing will not help us.

Compassion is the process that enables forgiveness to occur. It's the same when we show compassion towards someone even after they've made a wrong choice. Whether it's a case of our kids being rude or a complete stranger committing an act of violence, when we allow ourselves to see them *for who they really are deep down*, we are offering them love and compassion. This is when forgiveness has been extended.

I remember once, when I was speaking to a property management group, that one of the people in attendance had a massive breakthrough around forgiveness. It actually happened when I took the group through the exercises we did in chapters 1 and 2. He realized what was keeping him in a disempowered place, and it was that he had not truly forgiven someone for an incident that happened way, way back in his past. He told me he had been trying for years to forgive this person and knew he needed to but couldn't seem to make himself. As we've learned, it's really hard to talk ourselves into something, especially when we have strong feelings in our subconscious telling us otherwise. With the deeper mindset work we did during the exercise, he was able to actually shift those heavier feelings and let them go.

He came up to me afterwards in tears and just filled with gratitude for being able to finally let it go. It was such a beautiful moment, and it still brings me to tears as I share this story with you. It's this work that is just so powerful and far-reaching in our lives. It is this work that truly impacts every single person we come into contact with and impacts every single decision we make. I can't think of anything more powerful.

As we close this chapter, please forgive yourself.

Forgive yourself for judging your body.

Forgive yourself for not being where you want to be in your business.

Forgive yourself for not spending as much time with your kids as you would have liked.

Forgive yourself for judging other people.

Forgive yourself for judging yourself.

Forgiveness is a lifelong process, and we want to forgive

ourselves when we fall off track because inevitably we will. It's human nature, and these old patterns have been in place for a long time. Forgiveness starts with you, then it extends out to others. It's what will set us free.

COACH APPROACH

1. Think of a person or situation you would like to forgive but have not been able to. Pull up the memory in your mind, and answer the following questions.

2. Is the image of the memory a still, like a photograph, or is it moving and fluid, like a movie? How big is the image? Where is the location of the image? For example, is it a few feet in front of you, or is it far away in the distance? Are you seeing this image in colour or in black and white? Are there any sounds or smells associated with this image? If so, where is the location, and what is the nature of the sound or smell? Are there any other relevant emotions or feelings? If so, where are you experiencing them in your body? Good job!

3. Now think of a time when you completely forgave someone. It can be for the simplest thing—for example, maybe your child talked back to you, and you completely forgave them because you knew they were having an off day. Think of a simple, easy example, where full forgiveness came quickly and fully without much effort. Pull up the memory in your mind and really focus on the emotions

and the energy surrounding this memory. Then answer the following questions.

4. Is the image of the memory a still, like a photograph, or is it moving and fluid, like a movie? How big is the image? Where is the location of the image? For example, is it a few feet in front of you, or is it far away in the distance? Is it in colour or in black and white? Are any sounds or smells associated with this image? If so, where is the location, and what is the nature of the sound or smell? Are there any other relevant emotions or feelings? If so, where are you experiencing them in your body? Good job!

5. Now we're going to do some really cool "Jedi mind tricks." In a moment, I want you to go ahead and pull up the first memory of the person or event you have not been able to forgive. We are going to swap out all the characteristics of that memory with what you identified in the second one, where you *have* forgiven someone. We are going to make the picture have the same characteristics as the second memory. For example, if the first memory was in black and white but the second was in vibrant colour, we are going to change the first one to being in vibrant colour.

6. Go ahead and do that now. Dig down deep. Pull up that first memory. And swap out all the characteristics associated with the second memory instead, paying attention to everything you identified (i.e., still or a movie, colour, location, size of the image, and any sounds or feelings that were important). If the first memory had sounds but the second one didn't, you will change it to a silent memory. Go ahead and do that now.

7. Fantastic job! Now think of that person or incident you were having trouble forgiving. It likely does not have as much of a charge. Notice how you're feeling about it *now*. We have just loosened its vicelike grip over you, which will allow you to completely let it go (or at least begin the process). Let's have compassion for yourself and all those involved as you move forward.

You are awesome! Thank you for doing this important work. Think about the future now and how this ongoing process of letting go will impact your life and even your business moving forward.

9

Abundant Soul-utions

A Call to Action

SAY HELLO TO THE BEST version of yourself! She has been waiting for you. That version of you who is loving, confident, and *unstoppable*. The version of you who can and will create abundance because she now knows, without a doubt, that she is a masterful cocreator with the universe, and it's her *birthright* to be happy. *Ahh . . . I love this work so much!*

What a journey we've taken together! In each chapter, we have explored principles and practices that you will be able to weave into the beautiful fabric of your own daily life, both in your personal life and in your business life. As you move forward now, as you prepare to embark upon and continue this exciting journey towards abundant *soul*-utions in every aspect of your life, let's examine the highlights of what you have learned.

* You have learned about the power of your beliefs and how they dictate every single decision in your life.

* You have learned that an empowered belief system, when nurtured and maintained, creates a powerful energy that is released into the universe, and more of that vibration is then reflected back to you.

* You have learned that taking care of yourself makes you more resourceful and solution oriented.

* You have learned that when you clear out the physical, emotional, financial, and spiritual clutter in your life, you create the space to receive all the goodness the universe has waiting for you.

* You have learned where people-pleasing and the constant desire for perfectionism comes from and how you already are enough at your core.

* You have learned that it's okay to say no to what doesn't serve you and yes to what makes you happy.

* You have learned there is a whole universe supporting you and cheering you on and that you have this support system at your disposal at all times to create true love and abundance.

* You have learned what it really means to fully forgive and how to let go of your heavy, burdensome grievances.

* You have learned that self-care is actually self-love and that when you operate from this state of be-ing, it will always come back to you, allowing you to live a life of generosity, kindness, and joy.

When we practice self-love by tuning into our own needs and hearts' desires, we place ourselves in the highest frequency possible: the frequency of *love*. In this place, there is no fear, no doubt, and no worry. Here is the place where we simply give and receive love. Think about when you are so filled with joy, how much this joy ripples out like waves towards others. You are happy, loving, confident, and abundantly filled up. When we operate from this place, we are operating from our purest form, from the best and highest versions of ourselves that we can possibly be. Where thoughts of abundance lead to more thoughts of this nature and where ideas and *soul*-utions flourish. Where we are truly dancing with the universe, flowing and cocreating. It is the best place to *be*. It is receiving at the highest level. Where we allow ourselves to receive love not only from others and the universe but also from (and for) *ourselves*. In this place, we can give love and receive love, both, freely, without blockages or impediments. And the way we do it is through self-care.

Instead of always giving (doing), we have to create a balance so that we can allow ourselves to receive as well. That's what love is all about, isn't it? Love is about reciprocity. A beautiful balance between giving and receiving. It's what most of us, especially women who are born nurturers, tend to have the toughest time with. We therefore have to *create* the time and make the effort to receive, which could be as small as receiving a compliment or asking for help. It's when we don't allow ourselves to receive that we become resentful, overwhelmed, and stressed. And we know by now that we definitely cannot manifest what we really want from this low-energy place. That's why we have to confront and then dismantle all the outdated beliefs that tend to run the show and veer us off-track. We are more aware now of the dangerous paths that our ego and our subconscious thoughts can steer us. This heightened awareness is empowering and invigorating!

The practice of self-care raises our vibrational level, strengthens our energy, and deepens our connections. It empowers and uplifts our state of mind. It allows us to become more resourceful, more resilient, more inspired, and more successful. It allows us to soar to our highest heights while still keeping our feet firmly rooted on the ground.

Do we still get occasionally tripped up by listening to the ego more often than we should? Sure. We are human after all. But as we practice these truths and strengthen our belief in them, the *voice* of the ego becomes quieter. We see it for what it is, and we don't let it stop us. We have a faith and trust in something bigger than ourselves that is unwavering, that is always there for us, and that is waiting for us to meet it halfway. That's all it takes. Where we surrender our ego-based thoughts and accept a higher-level thought system, a thought system that will always show us the truth *if* we will listen. Where our own inner guidance system is the connection to our greatest source, with our intuition leading us there. As we strengthen and practice trusting this intuitive knowing, we realize the answers to all that we want are truly inside us. With self-care and therefore self-love being the way to get there. When we operate from this place, we are truly limitless. This is the place where solutions are abundant because they come from our *soul*.

I created the term *abundant soul-utions* out of a property investment, funnily enough, and it will forever have a special place in my heart. During the height of the COVID-19 pandemic, I started taking really long walks. I had always walked our dog and enjoyed being in nature, but these walks quickly became my saving grace (literally—our dog's name is Grace), and these walks were what kept me sane and grounded. They started increasing in length and duration quickly. I could have probably walked for days; it felt so good. I just had so much clarity, and my connection to source strengthened tenfold. It was inspiring and motivating and helped me not become a victim to the dire circumstances unfolding around us.

During one of my walks, I just *happened* to walk past a lot that was for sale. I started calling it the "magical fairy lot" because it looked (and felt) like something out of a botanical garden, with even the neighbours lovingly referring to it using that descriptor. It was a double lot, with an older home on one lot and basically a forest on the other. It was filled with trees and plants, various walking trails, and even a koi pond. It was indeed magical, and I did, without a doubt, want it. This was the dream, the desire, and the goal, that helped get me through the COVID-19 years.

I spent hours, and I mean hours, dreaming about this lot, planning, visualizing, and researching to make it happen. It was an expensive property and was almost within reach. Lengthy calls with a good friend who is a real estate agent ensued, and I learned more than I ever thought possible about what it takes to get a lot ready to build a house and then even more about the actual building process. A developer had purchased the land when the elderly owner passed, had split it into two lots, and planned to build two amazing homes on each. The plans were beautiful. But in the end, something felt off. All the trees and plants were cleared out of the magical fairy lot. I was still talking myself into it because a lot of that size is very rare in the tiny Southern California beachside community we live in with every space being maximized to the fullest. Also, the plans for this new house were incredible, with lots of outdoor living and space. But my husband had a gut feeling that something was off. After pouring hours and months of time and energy into this project, I was disappointed we weren't moving forward with it, but there was no convincing him, no matter how hard I tried. Well, postcompletion, the house on the neighbouring lot completely towers over the home we were looking at into not only the home itself but also the backyard and patio. There is little privacy. Also, the pool pump for the other house was placed right by the only ocean view deck of the home we were interested in. Imagine paying a fortune for this view, only to end up with a ton of unexpected noise disrupting your place of peace and tranquillity. A medium told me we would love that house but that something relating to the plumbing would be extremely expensive to fix. *Hmmm*, that's a story for another day, but it did prove my husband's *gut feeling* to be true. So that place was out, *but* the process ignited a new dream instead.

Along the way of my shenanigans, my husband reminded me that it was my dream to move by the ocean, which, of course, he loves and was on board with, but really it was my dream. (Dreams have to start in the heart of one person before they can spread to others, right?) His dream, on the other hand, was to have a place by the mountains. He loves to snowboard and even spent time living in Whistler, Canada, living the life of a *ski bum* back in the day. He shared that he would rather put our efforts into another home in the mountains. Well, he didn't need to tell me twice. I was in, and I was *on it*. I'm still not sure he expected such a fast turnaround, but hey, that's what I do. When I'm inspired, look out!

Just days later we decided to purchase a place in an area we fell in love with during a camping trip at the beginning of the COVID-19 pandemic, in Lake Tahoe. I have seriously never seen a lake like it. With its beautiful sapphire and turquoise blues and crystal-clear water. It's 6,000 feet above sea level, and you can still see snow on the mountains in the summer. It also doesn't freeze over, so you have these incredible lake views while skiing at any of the fifteen ski resorts that surround it.

Unfortunately, we were putting in offers at the peak of the surge in housing prices that ensued with the pandemic. Who would have thought? Well, we lost out on about nine houses. But then the market started to slow ever so slightly. And we ended up getting something for less than any of the other offers we put in. Even the agent we worked with couldn't believe it. But every single step miraculously showed up. From the home being the perfect one for us, to the price, to negotiating a credit, to us even doubling on other property investments we had that went toward this purchase just in time; in fact, one sale closed the same day *this* one closed. It was incredible! And we attracted *all* the right people, even when we were told by multiple sources just how hard it would be to find great people in such small mountain towns. Well, I went on to meet the most amazing cleaning staff and reliable house manager, negotiated an unheard-of partnership with a property management company, and even had our own contractor from San Diego drive all the way up there to complete a full remodel in just six short weeks! (He is still one of my favourite people in the world. We speak different languages, but his loving heart can easily be felt in his smile and kind nature. He is one of those people who would do anything for you and is one of the most hardworking I know.) Our vibe attracts our tribe! I even had our new place rented within the first two months of purchasing it. It all happened in record time.

As we sat at one of our favourite restaurants overlooking Lake Tahoe before the house closed, my husband wasn't sure it was all going to work out. I looked down my nose through my rose-coloured glasses (literally, my sunglasses have a pink tint) and said, "Abundant *soul*-utions, Jay, abundant *soul*-utions." Insert a little spiritual humour. We were being shown they very best solutions through our intuition to make the very best conclusion come to fruition.

Literally every step we'd taken on this journey had worked in our favour. Every single person we encountered had been the *right* person to help us advance and fulfil our dream. Everything aligned. And just a year after we purchased it, our property value went up 68 percent! And what was I affirming, and manifesting, the entire time in those days and weeks before we went to closing? What was the powerful prayer I was uttering? *Dear God, the universe, and the Holy Spirit, please help this go through if it will be a good short- and long-term investment and if it will be a great place for our family to enjoy.* This prayer continued to flow from me all the while, with my intuition guiding me every step of the way.

I'm sharing this story in detail because it's often the inspired *act* of manifesting that gets missed. Unfortunately, people just don't seem to recognize each step as being part of the bigger whole that will lead them towards what they are wanting to create. Each and every step counts. Every single step, no matter how big or small, is part of the bigger result. We must become an expert at spotting not only the bigger opportunity presenting itself but also all the smaller opportunities that will bring the bigger opportunity to fruition. Each incremental step must be seen as the opening that will ultimately propel us forward. Every tiny step we make guides us that much closer to fulfilling our dream, whatever that dream happens to be.

The other important piece to all of this is persistence. Once we make a decision to go for something, we have to see it through no matter what. We have to be willing to stay the course. It's this persistence, and an unwavering mindset to refuse to take no for answer, that acts as a catalyst and makes things *happen*. As I said before, where there's a will, there's a way. If you can dream it, per universal law, you can achieve it. So you have to keep saying yes. Don't listen to the voice of the ego that tells us to stop. To turn around. To go back. To choose an easier, safer route. As we've learned during our journey, the ego will try to deceive and derail you every step of the way. Does it mean we can't course correct? No. Look at how that first magical fairy lot led to landing us amongst the beauty in Lake Tahoe instead. Both achieving the ultimate intention of being in nature. You just need to be willing to trust your instincts and stay curious. Curiosity keeps us out of righteousness. When we appreciate and embrace the fact that we don't know all the answers, we can remain in a state of wonder and curiosity, and this allows us to allow ourselves to be shown the way. There is a surrender involved. And this surrender is what will allow our hearts' desire to come to fruition.

The people I interact with have gotten to know this about me, and it's why I'm always getting offered jobs by the people I work with, from real estate agents to mortgage brokers. Because I *get it done*. And I'm not tooting my own horn; I just really want to illustrate this is what it takes. You have to be willing to allow yourself to be shown new depths and new ways of making things happen that you never thought possible. You have to be willing to not let the ego's nos bog you down, not when there is a whole universe saying yes. The stand we're taking is against the ego.

Remember that the *how* is not up to us, but the trusting, the taking definitive action, and the maintaining a drive to keep going are.

This, my friends, is where hustle meets inspired action. Hustle is really more about operating from a place of fear, and inspired action is about operating from a place of love. When we're inspired, it doesn't feel like work, and we just do what we need to do to make things happen. It can become a slippery slope, though, with falling into old patterns of taking on too much.

This is why we need to realize when we take on new projects, even when inspired, that something has to go. Something has to give. We must be willing to put aside our perfectionist expectations and let the pool go green (you'll remember this reference from chapter 2) just for a minute. All those other projects will be there waiting for us when we're finished. This was when I knew my focus had shifted from coaching people privately to generating passive income through real estate. Quite honestly I was burned out from coaching, and something had to give. Even though real estate investing requires a lot of time and energy up front, it was all I wanted to focus on creating. Again, for me, there is something about cocreating these opportunities that I find fascinating. I continue to love teaching business owners the principles in this book but have passed the personal coaching baton to other amazing and capable coaches whom I've had the pleasure of taking through my coaching certification program. This brings me true joy and provides a way for me to give back everything I have learned about the coaching industry.

And how have I changed along the way? I've gone from the fear-based hustling of trying to make things happen, with always searching and trying to *get* something outside myself, to completely trusting and having faith that I'm always being shown the way, and that's it's all about turning *inward*. Where I've surrendered my own need for controlling how things will unfold to knowing, without a doubt, that everything is unfolding for me. Where I know I am worthy and deserving, where I know we're all connected, where I give myself copious amounts of time to practice self-care because I know it makes me a better and more resourceful version of myself. It's because of this mindset shift that I continued post-pandemic with my long walks. I continue my long walks, even today, because I'm certain they make me more grounded, calmer, more loving, more deeply connected, *and* more resourceful. Energetically, this is a beautiful place to be and one I continue to strive for and strengthen. Sure, I still get pulled into my ego-based thinking, like all of us, but my belief in the universe has tipped the scales, and its truth is now a stronger belief inside me than my ego's insecurities.

It's about trusting the truth now, this *universal* truth, that always has my back and leads me (and there to lead you too) to the most amazing miracles. It's about following this truth even when I'm not sure why and being confident enough to know that it will *always* work out favourably.

I've always allowed my intuition to guide me during coaching sessions, always been led by an inner *knowing* that gives me the tingles right afterwards, which tells me I'm onto something. I have learned to listen to, and trust, this inner knowing in *all* areas of my life; when my soul speaks to me, I have learned to listen to its voice rather than to the noisy voice of the ego.

Our intuition often speaks to us through seeing, hearing, or feeling something, such as seeing a sign, reading a passage in a book, having an interaction with another person, or allowing an inspired thought to come in during a calm moment. It then creates an idea inside us and an accompanying knowing that it's the truth, which can be felt in our bodies. This is what tells us we are on track. This is our intuition communicating with us. The way this response shows up in our bodies is different for everyone. For me, it tends to show up as *tingles* or just a deep knowing in my chest. It's a little difficult to explain with words because it's so feeling based and uniquely personal, but you will get to know exactly what it is for you as you practice tuning in and listening to it. It's what enables us to make conscious and aware decisions for ourselves without needing reassurance from others. It's truly liberating, knowing we have our own internal compass guiding and leading us.

It's there for us anytime regarding anything. Whether it's to find a *soul*-ution for a problem or something we're wanting to create, to those more mundane situations in our day-to-day lives like booking appointments or going grocery shopping. It all starts to become heart-warming and magical if we allow it.

One time when I was flying back from an event, my flight kept getting delayed. I went to the airport anyway to see if I could get on a different flight. When I arrived, there was one spot left. I was so happy to get that seat. It was with Southwest, where the seats are first come, first served, and while we were waiting to board, I heard another lady talking about how she got bumped, too, and now there was no way she would get a good seat and would for sure be stuck with a middle seat. I said a prayer and asked to be put in a window or an aisle seat and also that the flight be enjoyable.

I then noticed a couple in line but didn't think too much about it. Well, when I got on the plane, I saw that same couple and intuitively *knew* that was where I was supposed to sit, even though they were in the aisle and window seats. When I started making my way in, they switched since they were together and gave me the window seat! This is what I'm talking about—following the guidance there for us always that we so often tend to overlook.

Tuning in and trusting my intuition has taken me to new depths—and to new heights. It's become comforting to know I can connect with something larger than myself on the daily and for bigger creations, that it's there to guide us *all*, and to also be able to share the awareness of this guidance to others. We are all a part of that limitless, loving energy, so why not tune in to it and allow ourselves to be guided by it? That is true surrender.

My hope for you today is that you now *know* you are enough, more than enough. That you can trust yourself and your own inner compass. That it's okay to go after those big dreams and that you are a powerful cocreator with the universe. That you deserve—more than deserve but are also *required* to practice—an abundance of self-care. That you fully embrace the fact that receiving is just as important as giving. That when you do this, when you create this balance of giving and receiving, you are sending out the biggest ripple of love towards every single person in the universe, those you know and those you don't know who are waiting to feel your love.

So go on, sign up to help out with that school fundraiser or be the room parent, take on those new clients, read those personal development books, but do it with *intention* and conscious awareness. Make decisions that are grounded in what fills you up and not because they are a *should*. Should no more.

You are now equipped with the wisdom, the insight, and the practical tools you need to continue your *own* journey of abundant living. I will be cheering you on every step of the way. You are amazing!

My creative process: (Hint: This is what works for me and is a summary of what we've talked about during our time together. I encourage you to use them as a guide for creating too.)

1. Ask for what you want *clearly*.
2. Reject the limited beliefs that hold you back and jade your perception.
3. Affirm and act as if your new and empowered beliefs are real and energetic—because they *are*.
4. Practice self-care and in doing so raise your vibration.
5. Strengthen your trust in something larger than you.
6. Spot the opportunities, silence the voice of your ego, and learn to trust and rely upon your intuition.
7. Take inspired action and bring those opportunities to fruition.

Understand that this isn't the end; if anything, this is just the beginning. Yes, we have completed our literary journey, but you are just beginning your *own* journey now towards an inspired and empowered life. One where we are cheering each other on and ditching the ego's destructive judgement. One where we forgive and let go, surrender, and create. We are truly a community of kindred spirits now, filled with the wisdom, the knowledge, the tools, and the techniques we need to live alongside each other in gratitude and grace.

Keep practicing everything we went over, and continue to say yes to yourself. If you do this consistently and continually, you will, without a doubt, create and realize your true heart's desires. Love creates more love. Trust and have faith in the plan unfolding for you.

I would love to continue on this journey with you and for you to join me over at chrisatley.com/connecting.

As I mentioned, this is the end of one journey, the journey we have taken together as we've moved through the pages and chapters of this book, but it is also the beginning of another. It is the beginning of *your* journey towards joy, towards peace, towards love, and towards greater success in both your personal and professional life and, ultimately, towards a life filled with more abundance and self-love than you ever could have imagined.

Love,
Chris xox

REFERENCES

RESOURCE PAGE

To download the exercises mentioned in this book, along with the values game and money makeover retreat bonuses, visit www.chrisatley.com/resources for immediate access.

CHAPTER 1: HAM IN THE PAN
The Power of Beliefs

> *The Secret*, 2006, Rhonda Byrne, https://www.thesecret.tv
> *Empowered Future Exercise*, 2014, adapted from Terry Hickey from Belief Breakthrough Training, and Robert Dilts, Time Hallbom and Suzi Smith from Health Certification Training.
> *Timeline Exercise*, 2014, adapted from Terry Hickey from Belief Breakthrough Training.

CHAPTER 2: DON'T LET THE POOL GO GREEN
Self-Care Is Selfless

Decision-making Process, 2014, adapted from Terry Hickey from Belief Breakthrough Training.

Empowered Future Exercise, 2014, adapted from Terry Hickey from Belief Breakthrough Training, and Robert Dilts, Time Hallbom and Suzi Smith from Health Certification Training.

CHAPTER 3: CLEAR OUT THE CLUTTER
Creating Space for Growth

Clean Sweep, 2005, Coach U, https://www.coachu.com.

Money Exercises, 2014, adapted from Terry Hickey from Belief Breakthrough Training.

CHAPTER 4: IF IT'S NOT AN ABSOLUTE YES, IT'S A NO
Saying No and Setting Boundaries

Values Game, 2012, adapted from Jean Franzblau.

CHAPTER 5: DON'T TAKE THE BAIT
Managing Negative Energy

A Course in Miracles, 1976, by Helen Schucman, https://acim.org.

The Guest House, thirteenth century, by Rumi, translated by Coleman Barks (Penguin Classics, 2004).

Perceptual Positions Exercise, 2014, adapted from Terry Hickey from Belief Breakthrough Training.

CHAPTER 6: BE THE NUCLEUS, NOT NUCLEAR
The Perils of Perfection

Parts Integration Exercise, 2015, adapted from Jevon Dangeli, https://www.jevondangeli.com.

Forgiveness Exercise, 2014, adapted from Terry Hickey from Belief Breakthrough Training.

CHAPTER 8: FORGIVENESS
How Compassion and Love Shift the Life Dynamic

Forgiveness Exercise, 2014, adapted from Terry Hickey from Belief Breakthrough Training.

ABOUT THE AUTHOR

CHRISSY JAYE ATLEY is the CEO and founder of Decisions-by-Design and an award winning success coach and international speaker who has made it her life's mission to figure out the limitless potential we all have access to. As an NLP master coach, Chris has helped thousands of female entrepreneurs tap into their own inner resources to create the businesses and lives they have always imagined. She believes self-care is the key to connecting the dots between the subconscious mind and manifesting.

Chris speaks on stages around the world and has been featured by TEDx, the *Wall Street Journal*, and Bloomberg Radio, to name a few. She has a bachelor's degree in psychology from Wilfrid Laurier University and has attained many coaching certifications specializing in belief-breakthrough modalities. Canadian born, Chris now resides in a small beach town in San Diego, California, with her husband, two children, and dogs Gracie and Gordie.

CONNECT WITH CHRIS

Website
chrisatley.com

Resources
chrisatley.com/bookresources

Exclusive Connection
Join Chris to receive members-only content
chrisatley.com/connecting

Social Media
@chrisatley
@chrisatley
@chrissy.atley